THE CYBERSECURITY HANDBOOK

BOB SEEMAN

ISBN: 9798395677259 (Hardcover)
ISBN: 9798395676276 (Paperback)

Cover design by: CyberCurb

Publisher: CyberCurb, Vancouver

About the Author

Bob Seeman is the Managing Partner of CyberCurb and a Director of the Cyber Future Foundation Canada, an international collaboration of industry, public agencies and academia to build a more trusted and secure internet. Bob is also a Mentor at the Rogers Cybersecure Catalyst and Techstars.

He advises boards of directors on cybersecurity and also cybersecurity companies.

Bob has also published *On Trust, Risk, Power in Mistake, Ransomware Risk Mitigation for the Board*, and the foremost bitcoin-skeptic book, *The Coinmen*, which details how cryptocurrency is used for ransomware payments.

He is a California attorney, electrical engineer, and board director. Bob is a co-founder of RIWI Corp. which conducts data analytics, and he has advised governments internationally on technology and business issues. Previously, he was Head of Strategy for Microsoft Network in London, and a technical consultant to the European Commission.

Bob previously practiced administrative and regulatory law with the now Norton Rose Fulbright, a global law firm. He holds a Bachelor of Applied Science (Elec. Eng.) with Honours from the University of Toronto, a Master of Business Administration from EDHEC, and a Juris Doctor (J.D.) from the University of British Columbia.

For my future grandchildren

Table of Contents

Prologue

"There are risks and costs to a program of action – but they are far less than the long range cost of comfortable inaction."

John F. Kennedy

This book provides a high level introduction for non-technical executives of an organization to some of the issues surrounding cybersecurity. In particular, this book will convey why the organization should retain professional cybersecurity experts to advise on the particular requirements of the organization.

Companies must hire professional cybersecurity experts and rely solely on their professional advice. Cybersecurity involves a vast number of detailed and complicated issues. A detailed discussion would be many extremely thick books that would be almost unintelligible to a non-technical person. Cybersecurity is a profession that takes many years of study and hands-on experience. It continually evolves.

This book will help executives better understand: some of the key issues involved, why to hire cybersecurity professionals, what those professionals are recommending, and what questions to ask them. What follows is a non-technical introduction to the actual practice of cybersecurity.

Introduction

*"There is no castle so strong that
it cannot be overthrown
by money."*

Marcus Tullius Cicero

1.0. What is cybersecurity?

Over the last 30 years, the nature of value of an organization has significantly changed. The value has transitioned from being focussed on physical assets to a focus on digital assets. This digitization has transformed strategies and business models resulting in the digitization of corporate risk. In a digitally connected world, cybersecurity threats and incidents pose an escalating risk to companies.

The complexity of cybersecurity attacks ("cyberattacks") has grown significantly and continues to evolve. Increasingly sophisticated threats can overcome traditional protections and cybersecurity must keep up. Cybersecurity risks have increased for a variety of reasons, including the digitization of an organizations' operations, the prevalence of remote work, and the ability of cyberattackers to monetize cybersecurity incidents.

Cyberattacks affect companies of all sizes and all industries, and can have systemic effects on the economy.

For definitions of terms found in this book, please refer to *The Cybersecurity Dictionary* appendix of this book.

Cybersecurity involves people, processes, and technologies which prevent damage to, protect, and restore computers, electronic communications systems and services, and information to ensure information confidentiality, integrity, and availability.

- Confidentiality protects information from unauthorized access and disclosure, including theft of customer information.
- Integrity protects information from unauthorized modification, for example a change of the organization's payroll.
- Availability prevents disruption of the organization's access to information, including customer information.

Cybersecurity risks include unauthorized access, availability issues, impersonation, and other types of fraudulent claims. Organizations should consider potential impacts to the confidentiality, integrity, and availability of information, and information systems.

Risk assessment for cybersecurity involves: identification and estimation of degree of hazard, assessment of the company's exposure and vulnerability, and estimation of risk in terms of likelihood of threat occurrence and severity of outcome. Risk managers need to conduct risk assessments, and based on the information they obtain, make decisions about which risks are acceptable, tolerable, or intolerable.

Human factors are vital. Secure communication systems need to be user-friendly and not impose excessive cognitive burden on users. Research has shown that policies designed by security experts are often bypassed by employees because they demand too much effort and time and are, thus, ineffective. Cybersecurity management processes should be simple to use and designed such that mistakes are easy to fix. The idea is to fit the task to the human rather than the other way around.

Services should collect only essential data, minimize the replication and retention of data, cut down on linkages among the collected data, and avoid centralization of data. Data confidentiality can be achieved using cryptography. Privacy technology limits the information that is able to be leaked to potential adversaries, and ensuring, to the extent possible, that any data that are leaked cannot be linked to specific individuals.

Legal risk management involves understanding the laws and regulations that apply in all the jurisdictions in which an organization operates. The organization must consider the large number of laws and regulations, varying laws and enforcement authority across multiple jurisdictions, as well as the complexities of private law and regulatory systems. Juggling jurisdictional civil and criminal laws, risk assessment, human factors, online privacy, and threats from unknown adversaries is very challenging and costly to all organizations.

Organizations must weigh potential threats to cybersecurity, human factors, threats to user privacy, and laws and regulations when considering protecting the organization's future prospects and the privacy of their users.

"Today we were unlucky, but remember we only have to be lucky once. You will have to be lucky always."

The IRA to UK Prime Minister Margaret Thatcher after they failed to assassinate her.

Preparing for a Cyberattack

"It used to be expensive to make things public and cheap to make them private. Now it's expensive to make things private and cheap to make them public."

Clay Shirky, Writer

2.0. Introduction

By understanding the risks, an organization can better target its cybersecurity efforts. A cybersecurity program should provide reasonable assurance that an organization has made informed decisions related to information security. Risk evaluation looks at threats, vulnerabilities, likelihoods, and potential impacts that a cyberattack may have on an organization.

Every item of information cannot be protected against every cyberattack. Identify the organization's critical data, applications, and functions. Begin by listing all of the types of information that the organization has. What would happen to the organization if the information was made public or if the organization or its customers could not access the information?

Critical information may include financial records, proprietary assets, and personally identifiable information. To determine restoration priorities, identify which data or systems are most critical for operations and dependencies. More comprehensive security controls should apply to critical assets.

> *"As we know, there are known knowns; there are things we know we know. We also know there are known unknowns. That is to say, we know there are some things we do not know. But there are also unknown unknowns, the ones we don't know we don't know."*

Donald Rumsfeld, United States Secretary of Defense

Cyberattackers are not only motivated by money, but are also ideologically motivated "hacktivists" and nation-state actors. Some cyberattackers may attack the organization out of revenge, such as being fired, or just for the "fun" of causing chaos. Levels of cyberattacks from various cyberattackers are:

Serious

- Nation states, including Russia, China, USA and North Korea who engage in cyberespionage, theft, modification, destruction, and sabotage.
- Competitors who engage in cyberespionage, modification, destruction, and theft.

- Organized crime who engage in cyberespionage, fraud and theft.
- Terrorists who engage in sabotage and violence.

High

- Hacktivists who engage in cyberespionage, data theft, and sabotage.
- Disgruntled current or former employees who engage in misuse of data, physical theft, fraud and sabotage.
- Vendors or partners who engage in intentional fraud or theft.

Medium

- Thieves who engage in physical theft, cyberespionage, fraud.
- Mentally ill or irrational individuals who engage in physical theft or sabotage.

Low

- An individual with a specific limited purpose.

"Security is always excessive until it's not enough."

Robbie Sinclair, Head of Security, Country Energy, NSW Australia

A cyberattack can have a serious impact on an organization, often shutting down operations, causing financial loss, data breaches, and reputational damage.

The consequences include:

- Costs due to business interruption, decreases in production, and delays in product launches;

- Payments to meet ransom and other extortion demands;
- Remediation costs including liability for stolen information, system repairs, and incentives to partners to maintain the business relationship;
- Increased future cybersecurity protection costs, including increased insurance premiums;
- Lost revenue from theft of intellectual property and other proprietary information and the resulting failure to retain or attract customers;
- Litigation and legal risks, including regulatory actions and class action lawsuits;
- Harm to employees and customers, violation of privacy laws, and reputational damage; and
- Damage to the organization's competitiveness and share price.

2.1. Incident response plan

There are a variety of professional cybersecurity companies that provide incident response planning, protection and mitigation services to organizations. These include cybersecurity consultants, digital forensics, incident response companies and cyber insurance companies. Retain these companies as soon as possible to assist the organization to prepare an incident response plan.

An incident response plan helps to detect and respond to a cyberattack. The benefits include:

- reducing the impact of the cyberattack through better management of the response to the cyberattack;
- through practice, better decisions under the pressure of a real cyberattack;
- key actions are approved in advance allowing resources to be available and actions to be taken swiftly;

- a well-managed response with good communication builds trust with employees, customers and shareholders; and,
- learning from planning and practicing the plan helps to identify issues to be fixed.

An incident response plan must establish the authorities, roles, and responsibilities for the organization. Establish pre-authorizations to contract assistance and communicate with key incident response contacts.

Perform a business impact analysis to predict how an incident would harm the organization's operations, business processes, systems, and finances. Response efforts must prioritize the most critical systems and assets.

Create a cyber incident response team (CIRT) to assess, document, and respond to incidents, restore systems, recover information, and reduce the risk of the incident reoccurring. Include and specify the roles of cross-functional employees with a variety of qualifications.

Provide a central point of contact for the initial reporting of potential cyberattacks. Identify the internal and external key stakeholders who should be notified during a cyberattack. The stakeholders may include third parties, such as clients, managed service providers, suppliers, vendors, law enforcement and lawyers. Specify how, when, and with whom to communicate. Record all external contact information, such as private mobile phone numbers.

Prepare a draft statement in advance that can later be tailored to the specifics of the cyberattack. Cyberattacks can jeopardize the organization's reputation. Therefore, the communications plan must be implemented swiftly to enable stakeholders to enact their own incident response plans.

Print the plan out on paper, put it in a binder and distribute copies to all members of the CIRT. When a cyberattack happens, having an electronic incident response plan on the system will likely not be of any assistance.

Conduct a practice exercise to ensure all participants are aware of their role and required actions. Develop a training program for employees to ensure everyone is aware of their roles, and responsibilities in the case of a cyberattack.

"Those who do not archive the past are condemned to retype it!"

Simson Garfinkel and Gene Spafford,
Practical UNIX Security

2.2. Backups

One of the most important risk mitigation measures is a system data backup plan. Ensure that there are multiple copies of a backup of the entire system data stored offline and also in the cloud through a cloud service provider ("CSP"). A CSP may be Google, Microsoft, or Amazon Web Services (AWS).

Malware is malicious software designed to infiltrate or damage a system, or steal or harm use computing resources, without the owner's consent. Malware is intended to perform an unauthorized process that will have adverse impact on the confidentiality, integrity, or availability of an information system. Forms include ransomware, virus, spyware (spying), adware (advertising), worm, and Trojan horse.

Ransomware is a form of malware designed to block access to a computer system or data, often by encrypting data or programs on systems to extort ransom payments from a victim in exchange for decrypting the information and restoring the victim's access to their system or data.

Ransomware encrypts backups since the cyberattackers do not wish the organization to restore from backups and avoid having to pay the ransom. The cyberattackers wish to get paid. If the ransomware spreads to backups, it is not possible to restore and recover systems and data from the backup. Backups connected to the network, that is online or in the cloud, are susceptible to being infected with ransomware.

Offline backups provide protection against cyberattacks. "Offline" backups are backups that are only connected to the system (i.e. online) during the backup process. Use multiple backups stored offline and backup frequently so that data is always as up-to-date as reasonable. Multiple backups should be physically stored in multiple locations.

Regularly test both the backups and the restoring from backup processes. Ensure that the backups are ready to use to recover quickly from a cyberattack. Regularly conduct a full, encrypted backup of the data. Encryption makes electronically stored information unreadable to anyone who does not have the correct password or key. Encryption uses cryptography to convert plain (readable) text into cipher (unreadable) text to prevent anyone but the intended recipient from reading that data. Therefore, if only the encrypted backups are stolen, the cyberattacker will not be able to access or publicly leak sensitive information.

In addition, conduct an automatic incremental (differential) backup even more frequently. This type of backup only records any changes made since the last backup. Therefore, it is fast and can be efficiently performed more frequently.

Dispose of old backups, computers and computer storage media safely. Organizations may sell, throw away, or donate old computers and media. When disposing of old computer equipment, first electronically erase (wipe) them by completely writing over the entirety of all storage devices a sufficient number of times. Storage devices include internal and external hard drives, solid state drives or other removable media such USB memory sticks. In addition, physically destroy the drives and media.

> ## *"The software industry is really one of the only organizations where you can knowingly build a defective product and push it out to a potential buyer and the buyer assumes all the risk."*
>
> Jerry Davis, Chief Information Security Officer

2.3. Patch operating systems and applications

A vulnerability ("error") in any software application, including operating systems, or software installed on a system could provide the method for a cyberattack.

Software vendors provide patches to correct security issues and improve functionality. Check the operating system, and software regularly for updates. Patch and update applications regularly, including:

- Bug fix patches which repair functionality issues;
- Security patches which address security vulnerabilities; and,
- Feature patches which add new functionality to the software.

Patch servers connected to the internet first. Also prioritize patching software that processes internet data, including web browsers, browser plugins, and document readers.

Scan the hardware, software, and operating system for vulnerabilities. Have a process for receiving and addressing reports about security vulnerabilities. When vulnerabilities arise, fix them quickly.

2.4. Access control

Determine who should have access to what part of the organization's system. Do not allow any non-senior technical employee to have access to all of the system. Allow employees to access only those systems and information required to perform their work. For example, financial, personnel, inventory, manufacturing can each generally be separate systems in large organizations. Employees should have access only on a "need to know" basis.

Access control is the process of granting access to the system only to authorized users, programs, processes, or other systems. Use separate user accounts, each with limited access, to limit access to personally identifiable information or to control access to particular databases.

Apply the principle of least privilege: only provide employees with access to the functions and privileges necessary to complete their tasks. Remove special access privileges when users no longer require them.

Decommission and delete user accounts when someone leaves the organization.

If a cyberattacker gains access to an administrative account, they can use the elevated privileges, i.e. "all-access", to affect the organization's operating environment, attack the network, and access sensitive information.

"Passwords are like underwear: you don't let people see it, you should change it very often, and you shouldn't share it with strangers."

Chris Pirillo, Entrepreneur

2.5. Password management

Require individual user accounts for each employee. Set up a separate account for each user, including any contractors. Require that strong, unique passwords be used for each account. All employees must use accounts without administrative privileges to perform typical work functions.

Use of strong passwords will limit cyberattackers from being successful. Good passwords consist of a random sequence of letters (upper case and lower case), numbers, and special characters, and are at least 12 characters long. Insist on complex and unique passwords. Passwords like "121212" or "qwerty1" are not much better than no password at all. Cyberattackers use automated programs for "brute force attacks" by automatic entry of millions of combinations of characters in repetitive login attempts until they successfully guess a password. Therefore, restrict the number of login attempts.

Passphrases are preferable to passwords. However, most systems are currently configured to require a username and password to grant access. A sample passphrase might be "Fence8SoccerHappy%Bell". It is easy for a user to remember a picture of this passphrase in their mind. Passphrases are strong. Not only are they long, but they use capital letters and symbols. A passphrase is also easy to remember and type. People do not need to write them down and store them insecurely as is, unfortunately, too often done with passwords.

Train employees to never provide their username or passwords to others. Employees should also not use the same or similar passwords for both business and personal accounts. Therefore, if a personal account password is compromised that same password cannot be used by the cyberattacker on the business system.

Strong passwords/phrases are not enough to prevent a cyberattacker from gaining access. Implement multi-factor (i.e. method) authentication ("MFA"). A simple MFA is a text message to a phone. Text messages, however, are not secure and attackers can also remotely take over a phone number. A much better MFA is a specific hardware key or fob that is inserted into a computer or device. Smartphone authentication apps are also good. 2FA is two factor authentication, e.g., a password plus only one other method. 2FA is a form of MFA. MFA can require more that two factors, i.e. a password, a fob, *and* an eye scan.

In conjunction with MFA, use a password manager to remember and secure passwords required to access a system. However, password managers place all passwords into one place which may be lost or compromised. Compare password managers before implementing. Ensure the password manager encrypts all passwords stored on it. Use a strong password on the password manager itself and change that password regularly.

> *"I think computer viruses should count as life. I think it says something about human nature that the only form of life we have created so far is purely destructive. We've created life in our own image."*

Stephen Hawking

2.6. Perimeter defences

Perimeter defences protect the boundary between two network security zones through which network traffic is routed. Firewalls, anti-virus and anti-malware software can protect this boundary. Firewalls can be used to block unwanted traffic such as known malicious communications or browsing to inappropriate websites. Install a hardware firewall between the network and the internet and ensure antivirus software is installed on the firewall.

Protect particularly sensitive data by storing it in a separate and secure place on the system. This way, cyberattackers cannot use one network to connect to and access personally identifiable information on other corporate networks. Not every computer in the system needs to be able to communicate with every other one. Segment the network to ensure sensitive and high value information is in a different zone.

Use network segmentation to separate various business unit or departmental networks within the organization and maintain a separation between information and operational technology. This segmentation will assist to contain the impact of a cyberattack. Network segmentation can be breached through user error or violation of policies, such as connecting removable storage media, including USB sticks, to multiple network segments.

Consider also installing an intrusion detection system and intrusion prevention system, which devices analyze network traffic at a detailed level to monitor the network for malicious activity and can provide greater protection. Implement an intrusion detection system to detect "command and control" activity and other potentially malicious network activity that occurs prior to a cyberattack. A command and control server is a computer on the internet used by cyberattacker which is used to send commands to systems compromised by a cyberattack and to receive stolen data.

Ensure that users that access the network remotely do so using the organization's virtual private network (VPN). A VPN acts as a secure tunnel through which to send and receive data on an existing physical network. Using a VPN provides a secure connection between two points, such as a remote laptop and the organization's system.

Common services such as Remote Desktop Protocol (RDP) allow remote access to the system. RDP is normally used by the IT department to remotely fix computer issues. However, cyberattackers often gain initial access to a system through exposed and insecure remote services. Therefore, it is recommended to disable ports and protocols that are not being used for a business purpose, such as RDP.

Network security is only as strong as the weakest security on a computer with remote access to it. If an organization permits remote login to the system by a customer, it must first assess the cybersecurity of that customer.

2.7. Monitoring, logging and alerting

Implement continuous monitoring of the networks to establish a baseline for acceptable activity patterns within the organization. Access to the monitoring logs (records) should be limited to only to those who need to know.

As part of monitoring, implement automatic alerting for anomalies in activity patterns to be flagged and reviewed. Potential vulnerabilities and events that need risk mitigation action may also be identified this way. Alerts indicate something out of the ordinary has occurred and the organization can then review them and consider what, if anything, should be done to mitigate any risk.

After a cyberattack, logs provide insight about how the cyberattack occurred and what measures can be implemented to better protect against further cyberattacks.

2.8. Penetration testing

In a penetration test (pen test), a cybersecurity professional attempts to breach a system's security, using tools and techniques that a cyberattacker might use.

Some vulnerabilities are commonly known. For example, web applications are commonly vulnerable to Structured Query Language (SQL) injection attacks.

This vulnerability can lead to use SQL attacks to gain access to databases containing consumer information. That risk could have been avoided by pen testing for commonly-known vulnerabilities.

"Phishing is a major problem because there really is no patch for human stupidity."

Mike Danseglio, Microsoft program manager

2.9. Email protection

Usually malware is attached to, or embedded in, emails, texts, or social media posts that pretend to be legitimate ("phishing"). Links and attachments may look legitimate but, in fact, download malware. Phishing fools a person into clicking on a malicious link or attachment. The click causes the malware to execute computer commands. Cyberattackers often use the identities of third parties to send spoof (masquerade) emails to target organizations.

Do not click on a link or open an attachment that was not expected. Telephone the sender to verify that they sent the email and ask them to describe what the attachment or link is. An alternative is to forward (not "reply" since the reply email address may be faked) the email to the person who purportedly sent the email (using their email address already in your address book) and ask them to reply for verification. Avoid clicking on links. Instead of clicking, consider using a search engine to search for the purported legitimate document or website and then click on the search engine result instead.

If a user considers that, despite the above advice, they must click, before clicking, hover over the link to see the actual web address to which the click will go. That address is usually shown at the bottom of the browser window.

As much as possible, require separate devices and email accounts for personal and business use. Personal computers may be less secure than business systems. Personal devices might be used to access untrustworthy websites and have untrustworthy applications installed, such as games, which are not required for work. Untrustworthy websites and applications can create vulnerabilities.

Consider implementing security measures to protect the organization's internet domain names from email spoofing (masquerading by a cyberattacker). Such measures will prevent the delivery of malicious messages sent in relation to the domain names. Specifically, the organization should implement a Domain-based Messaged Authentication, Reporting and Conformance (DMARC) policy and verification to protect the domains used for email from being spoofed.

Email filters remove emails known to have malware attached. Install anti-phishing software which will block phishing emails. Implement filters to filter out emails with known malicious indicators, including known malicious subject lines, and block certain suspicious Internet Protocol (IP) addresses.

To phish users, cyberattackers may also use compromised email accounts associated with, or spoof the identity of, third-parties with whom the organization has a trusted relationship.

2.10. Web filters

Malware can infect a system simply by a user visiting an infected website. Such a "drive-by download" occurs when a user unknowingly visits a malicious website where malware is surreptitiously and automatically downloaded and installed. Similarly, "malvertising" adds malware to legitimate online advertisements. If a user clicks on an advertisement, the malware enters an organization's system.

Block employees from visiting websites associated with cybersecurity threats. Such blocking will assist to prevent employees from accidentally downloading malware. Many web browsers allow web filtering which notifies the user if a website might be malicious malware and the web browser may prevent the user from accessing that website.

The Domain name system (DNS) is the address book for the internet used for both human-initiated actions, such as visiting a website, and computer-initiated actions. The organization should implement protective DNS to block employees using corporately issued devices from visiting potentially malicious domains on the internet. Protective DNS identifies malicious domains using a blocklist, which is a listing of prohibited domains and IP addresses.

2.11. Third parties

A supply chain attack occurs when a cyberattacker infiltrates a third-party service or supplier infecting their and their customers systems with malware, often through a seemingly normal software update.

Cyberattackers also exploit the trusted relationships that the organization has with third parties and managed service providers (MSPs). They may target MSPs to compromise their clients. A cyberattack on an MSP can easily affect their clients. A cyberattacker may use the MSP's network connection and access to the organization to propagate malware.

An organization must, therefore, consider the risk management and cybersecurity practices of third parties or MSPs that it relies upon. Select third party providers that are able to implement appropriate security measures and monitor that that are meeting the requirements. Verify the security expectations specified in contracts with service providers.

2.12. Cyber insurance

The first cyber insurance policies were designed to handle damages arising only from errors and omissions respecting technology. As organizations digitized their operations, cyber insurance companies expanded coverage to include cyberattacks and the associated risks of data breach and business interruption.

Today, cyber insurance covers certain losses due to a cyberattack and may include assistance to respond and recover from the cyberattack. Cyber insurance companies may also provide cybersecurity expertise, help identify vulnerabilities, help with actions to take before and after a cyberattack, and help to investigate a cyberattack.

The existence of cyber insurance has the potential encourage cyberattackers to launch cyberattacks – since victims may be more likely to pay if they have insurance. Cyberattackers, therefore, may target organizations because the organizations are suspected to have cyber insurance. At the same time, insurance providers generally require that their clients have strong cybersecurity practices, which better practices will help to protect the clients from cyberattacks.

Insurers have identified risk factors and developed the expertise to help organizations better secure themselves. Increased scrutiny of prospective insurance buyers is designed to incentivize the organization to make appropriate security investments and become prepared. To better measure an organization's cybersecurity risk, some cyber insurers are using third-party cybersecurity companies to conduct assessments. Insurers may deploy in-house security and risk engineering expertise to help insured organizations. A number of insurers have established or acquired cybersecurity companies to provide managed threat detection, incident response, or security consulting services to clients.

Insurers incentivize organizations to become more secure using strategies that include reduced claim limits for coverage; the joint assumption of a risk by the insured and insurer; and premium increases.

Insurers may refuse to offer insurance coverage to organizations that do not first establish an appropriate level of cybersecurity. Accordingly, the organization may, for example, need to confirm that it follows a recognized cybersecurity framework, has deployed multi-factor authentication (MFA), or is properly managing the risks associated with remote access. Organizations that lack a minimum level of cybersecurity may be uninsurable.

The insurance may include the assistance of a third-party cybersecurity professional if there is a cyberattack. The professional would provide incident response expertise and a recovery strategy. They may help lead the organization's response and recovery process.

Common components of a cyber insurance policy include:

- Incident response costs
  - o The cost of responding to a cyberattack, including forensics and experts; internal

response costs; legal costs; and costs related to restoring systems.

- Data privacy liability
  - The cost of dealing with and compensating third-party individuals whose information may have been compromised by the cyberattack.
- Data recovery costs
  - The cost of recovering data or software.
- Business interruption loss
  - Lost profits or extra expenses incurred due to the unavailability of systems.
- Regulatory defense
  - Provides coverage for fines, penalties, and defense costs respecting regulatory actions including privacy laws.
- Cyber ransom / extortion
  - The cost of ransom / extortion response expertise to vet and evaluate all possible options for recovery, and, if required, negotiate and execute any ransom payment.
- Reputational damage
  - Loss of revenues arising from loss of customers or reduced number of transactions.
- Network liability
  - Third-party liabilities for malware passing through an organization's system to a third party.
- Contingent business interruption loss
  - Costs of business interruption resulting from a cybersecurity failure of a third party such as a supplier.
- Technology errors and omissions liability
  - Coverage for third-party claims relating to failure to provide adequate technology.
- Financial theft and fraud
  - The direct financial loss arising from the use of computers to commit fraud or theft.

- Physical asset damage
  - Loss due to the destruction of hardware or other physical property.

2.13. Education and training

Have a cybersecurity user awareness and training program which trains employees in good cybersecurity practices. Have frequent discussions amongst employees. A system is only as secure as its weakest link. Generally, employees are the weakest link and a key part of how cyberattackers successfully launch a cyberattack.

Explain methods like phishing and how to identify malicious links. Provide guidance regarding identifying and reporting malicious activity or a suspected cyberattack. Encourage the reporting of incidents even if they turn out to be innocent. Conduct phishing tests for the entire organization to measure user awareness and reinforce the importance of identifying potentially malicious emails.

Warn about social engineering and test employees' cybersecurity knowledge. "Social engineering" is an attempt by cyberattackers to obtain access to personal or business information by fooling people. A common cyberattack involves a fake person, website, and/or email. A cyberattacker would research the organization in advance to learn names, and titles, and personal information. Then, the cyberattacker telephones or sends an email saying that she is another employee or business partner to convince a person at the organization to give her confidential information such as a password. Never respond to an unsolicited telephone call that asks for sensitive personal or business information. Employees should notify management if there is such an attempt.

Employees must be trained on information security expectations and the policies and procedures should be readily accessible to employees in an employee handbook or manual. All employees must sign a statement agreeing that they have read the policies and relevant procedures and that they will follow them. Employees must be aware of any penalties associated with the policies and procedures. Policies and procedures should be reviewed and updated at least annually. Whenever the policies are changed, employees should be educated about the changes and sign the updated policy. To protect the system and the organization, the key is *education* of the employees and *not* the paperwork.

Recovery from a Cyberattack

"In theory, one can build provably secure systems. In theory, theory can be applied to practice but in practice, it can't."

Marc Dacier, Professor

3.0. Introduction

After a cyberattack, how does the organization recover and get back to business?

It is essential to identify how the cyberattacker was able to enter the network, systems, and devices and to address the vulnerability immediately. Without identifying how the cyberattacker gained access and applying appropriate additional cybersecurity, cyberattackers may continue to exploit the same vulnerability.

What systems, accounts, and information did the cyberattacker access? This information helps to determine the extent of the damage, including the accounts that were compromised and what data may have been exfiltrated (stolen). The information will also help to control the cyberattack, implement the appropriate response, and successfully recover.

3.1. Containment and eradication

Determine which systems were impacted, and immediately isolate them from other parts of the system. Isolation prevents the cyberattackers from moving laterally to other parts of the system to preserve their access or deploy malware more widely. Disable the execution of the malware as soon as possible.

If unable to disconnect devices from the network or to temporarily shut down the network, turn off the devices to avoid further spread of the malware. Note that potential evidence stored in temporary device memory will be is erased when a device is turned off.

Despite the disruption to the organization, isolating the system from the internet is important. Isolation will temporarily remove the cyberattacker's access to the system. Cyberattackers can infiltrate a system and continue to have access to the system. Cyberattackers may monitor the organization's activity or communications to understand if their actions in the system have been detected. Therefore, assume the cyberattackers have access and use an alternative communication method such as email or telephone using devices not connected to the system ("out-of-band"). Therefore, the cyberattacker will not be able to learn from and counter the organization's incident response plans and recovery actions.

Examine the organization's detection or prevention systems for evidence of additional systems or malware. Identification may also involve audits of accounts, examination of data found in logging systems, and a forensic analysis of the system. Collect relevant logs, samples of malware, or other indicators of compromise. Try to preserve evidence that may be deleted, including system memory, Windows security logs, and data in firewall log buffers. Take an image (complete copy) and memory capture of affected devices.

Safely completely erase (wipe) by writing over the entirety of infected devices to remove the malware.

3.2. Rebuild

Before starting the restore process, run anti-virus diagnostics on the backup that will be used to make sure that it the most up-to-date backup which is not infected. Rebuild systems based on a prioritization of critical services, e.g., health and safety or revenue generating services.

Once the system has been rebuilt, reset passwords. Address the identified cybersecurity vulnerabilities, including applying patches, upgrading software, and taking other cybersecurity precautions previously omitted.

3.3. Pay the ransom?

This is the million dollar question. Often it is *literally* the million dollar question.

While many organizations oppose paying ransoms but, in the end, reluctantly agree to, they may not be aware of all the options. A common misunderstanding is that the only alternative to payment is to entirely rebuild the system. Rebuilding the system may be too costly or take too long for organizations that provide critical services that require immediate restoration. In many cases, alternatives exist between payment and a rebuild of the full network.

A cyberattack is a stressful, and potentially existential, event for an organization. The decisions about how to respond – including whether to pay the ransom – are made under great pressure. Organizations may make rushed decisions if they do not understand the consequences of paying a ransom and alternatives.

The organization must decide whether it should pay the ransom and hope that the attackers restore access and not publicly disclose any data. And hope it is. Criminals are, by definition, not trustworthy. Therefore, the organization must do everything possible to restore normal operations itself without paying the ransom.

Cyberattackers generally try to use time pressure to try to persuade victims to pay. However, often other options are possible. Backups of data might be accessible, allowing a victim to recover their operations. Also, a publicly available decryption key might already exist for the particular ransomware.

Victims of a cyberattack should engage a cybersecurity incident response company to assist in the process of advising on, and potentially paying, the ransom. Such companies include the cyber insurance provider, law firms, negotiation companies, threat intelligence, and forensic investigators. Negotiation companies communicate with the cyberattackers and try to lower the ransom payment demanded. Incident response companies, law firms, and financial institutions may also perform due diligence to ensure a payment would not violate government sanctions. In the United States, organizations that pay a ransom may violate of Office of Foreign Assets Controls regulations if they pay a terrorist entity. The companies would also investigate applicable insurance coverage, and whether there is a publicly available decryption key.

Factors affecting the decision to pay the ransom include whether there is cyber insurance, the quality of the data backups, and the estimated costs of the system downtime. Legal issues may also be relevant. Cyber insurance policies do not require a victim to pay a ransom. The decision to pay is the victim's.

Cyberattackers encourage organizations to pay the ransom by threatening to release stolen data to publicly to embarrass the organization. Victims are more likely to pay if they are concerned that their data will be made public.

The threat of public disclosure of the stolen data may also be made by the cyberattackers *after* the first ransom is paid in order to extort a *second* ransom. This ransomware technique is known as "double extortion". The cyberattackers demand a second payment in return for not disclosing the information to authorities, competitors, or the public. Double-extortion threats provide additional bargaining leverage beyond data encryption. Leaks can lead to the loss of intellectual property, brand damage, or initiate regulatory investigations.

There is also a triple extortion possible if the decryption key provided by the attacker does not completely restore the data. Never trust a criminal to provide the correct decryption key. Also, the encryption may not have been performed correctly so the files may not be able to be entirely decrypted or at all.

Further, quadruple ransom is possible if ransomware remains in the system or the cyberattacker still has access to the system. Even if no ransomware or access remains, the cyberattackers may re-target an organization which pays, since the organization is now a "mark" – the cyberattacker knows that it pays up. Therefore, it is essential to fix all cybersecurity issues immediately as part of recovering after a cyberattack.

Further extortion is possible if attackers harass or coerce the victims' clients with the threat to disclose the clients' confidential information.

Law enforcement and security experts advise that paying the ransom is not a good option. Half of victims who pay a ransom do not successfully recover their data.

3.4. Communicate

Coordinate with communications and public information personnel to ensure accurate information is shared internally with the organization and externally with the public.

Establish the likelihood of the confidentiality or integrity of the organization's data having been compromised and inform data managers and stakeholders of potential impacts.

Report the cyberattack to local law enforcement.

3.5. Recovery and post-incident activity

Post-recovery, conduct a lessons learned exercise to implement further mitigation measures and correct actions and strategies. Document the lessons from the cyberattack and associated responses to inform updates to the organization's policies, plans and procedures, and guide future activities. Revise the incident response plan accordingly.

Planning Long Ahead: Assessing and Managing Risk

"They've finally come up with the perfect office computer. If it makes a mistake, it blames another computer."

– Milton Berle, an American actor and comedian.

4.0. Introduction

With the reality of billions of connected digital devices, the potential impact of a cyberattack or disruption to digital infrastructure can become a matter of major significance. It is crucial that all organizations and individuals plan long ahead. They must understand and actively participate in assessing and managing cyber risk. Therefore, cybersecurity risk assessment and management is critical.

4.1. Risk assessment

Risk assessment has three components: (1) identification and estimation of degree of hazard, (2) assessment of the company's exposure and vulnerability, and (3) estimation of risk by combining likelihood of occurrence and severity of outcome.

"When the inventor of the drawing board messed things up, what did he go back to?"

– Bob Monkhouse, an English comedian.

4.2. Risk management

Risk management involves evaluating the information obtained from risk assessments and, based on this information, making decisions about which risks are acceptable, tolerable, or intolerable. The choices for managing risk may include mitigation, transfer (i.e. transferring the risk to another party by agreement with that party and/or obtaining insurance), or sharing of risk meaning that no one person bears the brunt (i.e. the cost of remediation.) Choices will depend on what has been called an organization's "risk appetite".

Four types of risk have been identified, each one requiring different risk management plans: routine risks, complex risks, uncertain risks, and ambiguous risks. Specific approaches to management of risk include a statistical analysis for routine risks, a cost-benefit analysis for complex risks, a precautionary approach for uncertain risks, and participatory decision-making for ambiguous risks.

The public perception of risk often differs from actual risk due to common cognitive biases such as a tendency to exaggerate dreaded risks that are rare and downplaying commonplace risks that are, indeed, common. It is important to align public perception with actual risk. Risk-benefit analysis is important.

Another way of structuring risk assessment is to consider the four core concepts of vulnerability, threat, likelihood, and impact. Vulnerability is an inherent weakness in a system that can easily lead to an undesirable outcome if it is exploited. Threat is the would-be exploit (cyberattack) by an attacker. Likelihood is the estimated probability that a threat will exploit a vulnerability, and impact is the negative effect of that happening.

"Good judgment comes from experience, and experience comes from bad judgment."

– Rita Mae Brown, an American feminist writer.

4.3. Risk governance

Risk governance is vital. It helps organizations make informed decisions regarding the potential risks that they face and how to manage them both before and after they occur. The initial process of risk governance involves a thorough examination of the context (how often and against whom are cyberattacks occurring), assessing risks and concerns (sophistication of employees, training of employees), characterizing those risks (identifying them and communicating them), managing them, and continually monitoring and refining the process to ensure that it is effective and current. The principles of risk governance ensure that decisions are made based on a clear understanding of the legal, social, organizational, and economic context, all of which changes with time.

A structured process of risk management is required, not random decisions that rely on intuition and bias. All employees must understand cyber risk. Training, behavior change, trust building, and stakeholder involvement are crucial. Rules about security routines, password complexity, confidentiality and frequent adjustment are bothersome for employees. Rather than being imposed, they need to be explained, discussed and willingly accepted. Every employee must ultimately be accountable for failure to accept regulations. Training needs to be reviewed, improved, and repeated. Ideally, failures in the risk governance process should lead to constant feedback and improvement. Individuals need to be able to freely report accidental policy breaches so that they can be corrected.

Some organizations tend toward technocratic risk management that is based on scientific evidence; some choose a decisionistic style that incorporates social and economic drivers of risk; and some organizations are more transparent than others, meaning that their decisions are based on input from stakeholders and are known to all stakeholders. The key to successful risk governance is to ensure that it is tightly coupled with day-to-day decision-making, such as health and safety, finances, and human resources. The cyber risk governance approach should be part of the operational culture of the company and be wholeheartedly adopted by everyone involved. The more inclusive and transparent the policy development, the more likely it will receive support and buy-in from stakeholders.

"Whoever is careless with the truth in small matters cannot be trusted with important matters."

– Albert Einstein, an absent minded genius. Many quotes attributed to Einstein are apocryphal.

4.4. Human factors and risk communication

Human factors such as employees not understanding the importance of confidential data and system security, not perceiving that they are at risk, and not following safe policies can and do impact security governance. Risk communication is crucial in addressing these challenges. It means involvement of all stakeholders, education, creating confidence that permits behaviour change, and leading by example. What needs to be communicated is a sense of responsibility and accountability in a culturally-sensitive and morally ethical context. For further detail, see the Human Factors chapter in this book.

It is important to create a company culture where people feel comfortable reporting issues and concerns, without fear of being penalized. Security works for everyone. It's important to note that completing awareness training does not always guarantee that graduates will comply with regulations. It is human to slip up or to be unknowingly taken in by guile.

4.5. NIST risk assessment guidelines

The US Government's National Institute of Standards and Technology (NIST) risk assessment guidelines capture the vulnerability, threats, likelihood and impact elements within what they refer to as the Prepare, Conduct, Communicate, and Maintain cycle:

- Prepare: Defining the purpose, scope, and assumptions for the assessment, as well as identifying sources of information about threats, vulnerabilities, and impact. Preparing also means determining the assessment approach to take and the amount of risk tolerance one is willing to assume.

- Conduct: Carrying out the assessment, analyzing the information, documenting the results and communicating them to stakeholders.
- Communicate: Determining who needs to be informed, what information needs to be shared, how it will be communicated, and communicating it. It also means obtaining feedback and incorporating it into the risk management process.
- Maintain: Continuous monitoring and updating of the risk assessment so that it reflects changes in the environment or context. Reassessment may be necessary. Also necessary is verifying that the risk management plan is being implemented effectively, and making changes whenever needed.

4.6. Vulnerability management

The vulnerability of software is important to assess and re-assess regularly. Automated tools can scan the network to identify vulnerable assets and generate reports that should be reviewed regularly to prioritize and schedule fixes. Factors like impact, visibility, and ease of exploitation need to be considered when prioritizing fixes.

The distinction between security and safety is important in the context of cyber-physical systems and the hardware and software systems used to operate industrial control devices (operational technology or OT.) While traditional IT security focuses on minimizing access, modification, and downtime within components and systems, OT risks demand focus on safety due to the impact of failure on worker and public safety. To mitigate these risks, a systems-driven approach to risk management is recommended, with the focus on high-level objectives such as avoiding harm and complying with regulations.

4.7. Security metrics

There are open questions about what features of a system to measure for security, how to measure them, and why they need to be measured. Good metrics should be easy and inexpensive to measure, expressed with cardinal numbers and familiar units, and relevant to one's business. Qualitative ratings such as high/medium/low are best avoided.

4.8. Incident management

Incident management is a crucial aspect of cybersecurity and risk assessment, management, and governance. Incident management involves responding to cyberattacks, minimizing their impact, implementing a remediation plan, and using the lessons learned to improve defenses and plan for the future.

4.9. Information sharing

Sharing information about cybersecurity breaches, while still considered taboo in many organizations, is becoming increasingly important as offenders increasingly collaborate and share intelligence about opportunities and vulnerabilities. Many industries, such as the financial and pharmaceutical sectors, have established information-sharing arrangements.

"There are worse things than getting a call for a wrong number at 4 am. It could be a right number."

– Doug Larson, a columnist.

Factoring-in Human Behavior

"To make a mistake is human, but to blame it on someone else, that's even more human."

5.1. Introduction

The principles for designing reliable cybersecurity are rooted in a knowledge of human behavioral sciences – psychology, forensics, and economics. We have learned that secure communication systems need to be user-friendly and not impose excessive cognitive burden on users. The number of security measures that a person or an organization needs to take have to be minimized as much as possible. The effort required to bypass a security measure should be substantially greater than the resources and potential rewards for the cyberattacker.

The failure of cybersecurity measures is not attributable to users being, as often said, the "weakest link". Rather, the failure lies in the security design that ignored factors such as usability and acceptability. Password policies highlight this issue. Research has shown that policies designed by security experts are often bypassed by employees and, thus, ineffective. Software developers also put in outdated mechanisms that have proven faulty. Findings such as these emphasize the need for a focus on human factors in the design and implementation of secure systems.

When users do not follow security policies, they are blamed for not understanding the risks or simply being too lazy. But non-compliance or "rule-bending" is just as often a result of a "Sophie's choice" (A choice where both alternatives carry negative consequences) between productivity and security, and choosing productivity because that is the more immediate organizational demand.

The typical response to non-compliance is security awareness and education, but this approach is not always effective. Human factors research has established that "fitting the task to the human" is more efficient than the other way around in terms of both cost and performance. Security awareness and training can play a role in improving security, but it should not be the first resort. Security must be usable, with usability being defined as the effectiveness, efficiency, and satisfaction of users achieving their goals. Security must work for people.

5.2. Usability

Criteria for assessing the usability of a system are:

- Effectiveness: The accuracy and completeness with which specified users can achieve their goals in a specific context.
- Efficiency: The resources (e.g. time and effort) expended in relation to the accuracy and completeness of the goals that one tries to achieve.
- Satisfaction: The comfort and acceptability of the system to its users and those affected by its use. It is a measure of the user's level of enjoyment and ease with the task.
- Capabilities and limitations of target users: Understanding the skills, knowledge, and abilities of users is crucial in designing security measures that are within their easy reach. Security measures should

align with the other goals and tasks that users need to perform routinely.

- Physical and social context: The context puts constraints on the ease of performing security tasks.
- The capabilities and limitations of the device: The device on which security measures are used can also play a role in their usability, e.g. screen size, processing power, and input methods.

Humans have general physical and mental capabilities and limitations, and tasks that exceed these capabilities will not succeed. Security mechanisms must not demand too much time or attention, and should be clearly and simply placed in front of the user to require a response, not be reliant on a user's memory.

5.3. Alarm fatigue

Alarm fatigue refers to a situation where users stop paying attention to security warnings due to the relatively high rate of false alarms. This situation is like the boy who cries "wolf", when the brain begins to classify repeated signals as irrelevant and filters them out before they reach consciousness. To avoid alarm fatigue, it is important to keep the alarm rate as low as possible and to only issue security warnings when necessary. At the time of issuing a security warning, explain why it is important and precisely what needs doing. The recommendation is to keep the false alarm rate below 10%. Above that percentage, it loses its effect. Suggested ways of doing this includes good technology support. Job rotation is also a good idea, although it is not always possible. With human beings, being what they are, once they begin dismissing alarms, it becomes difficult to turn the clock backward.

"Anyone who has never made a mistake has never tried anything new."

– Albert Einstein, one of the greatest and most influential physicists of all time.

5.4. Human memory

Memory is a key mental capability in humans and is divided into short-term memory (STM) and long-term memory (LTM). STM is used for temporary storage of information, like one-time passwords, but it has limited capacity and can only easily handle strings of up to 6 characters. Long-term memory is divided into semantic memory (LTM-SM) and episodic memory (LTM-EM.) The ability to recall information stored in LTM depends on how frequently it is retrieved. Infrequently used information stored in LTM-SM fades faster than information stored in LTM-EM because the latter is connected to personal history and emotions. Overloading the STM loop with long or alpha-numeric codes takes more time and has a greater likelihood of error.

To better cope with the memory issue, the following solutions are recommended: multi-factor authentication, password managers, or keeping strong passwords for longer periods.

5.5. Passwords

A knowledge-based authentication credential, such as a password, needs to be extremely difficult to guess.

Easier guesses for cyberattackers:

- Users usually pick passwords that are easy for them to recall, such as personally significant names or dates.
- When using images as credentials, users usually prefer stronger colours and shapes.
- When the images are pictures of humans, they will choose more attractive people.
- When using a location within a picture, people prefer obvious features.
- With a location-based system, people pick memorable locations; when choosing locations for a 4-digit PIN on a number grid, they choose locations on the grid that are next to each other and at an edge or corner of the grid.
- The order of the elements (e.g. letters, numbers, characters) of a credential is predictable. People who write languages that read left-to-right will choose the elements in that order.
- With finger swipe passwords, users generally choose from a limited number of shapes.

These biases in the selection of credentials result in easily guessable knowledge-based authentication, making it less secure. To reduce this risk, security systems can implement various measures such as randomizing the order of elements, offering a wide range of options to choose from, or using multiple elements to form a single credential. These changes increase the randomness of the system, making it more secure against guessing attacks.

Security policies have also restricted too obvious password choices, but these polices have increased the workload associated with password creation and recall, causing frustration and time lost in retrieval. Visible password strength "meters" have been used to guide password choices, but these meters can vary in accuracy. The workload associated with password creation can also increase with restrictions, and password strength meters. It is also important to consider the specific needs of different user groups, such as children, older citizens, and those with physical and mental conditions. The usability limitations of security mechanisms and their contribution to security fatigue must also be kept in mind.

"I changed my password to 'incorrect', so anytime I forget and enter the wrong thing, the computer tells me what it is."

5.6. User behaviour

Workarounds to security measures, like writing down passwords, occur because people want to ensure effective completion of their tasks and protect business productivity. The repeated effort and disruption of entering a password many times a day can lead to negative effects such as installing mouse-jiggling software to avoid screen lock.

The aim must be to reduce the burden of security tasks on users. This can be done by automating security, minimizing the need for explicit human action, triggering security mechanisms only when necessary, and designing systems that are secure by default. As people tend to prefer physical tasks over mental tasks, the design should aim to reduce mental workload as much as possible.

To reduce security compliance fatigue, security specialists need to discuss with line managers and business leaders the time and budget available for security tasks. Making security mechanisms smarter and less restrictive reduce compliance fatigue. Access to efficient security recovery and support services reduces the need for workarounds.

Multi-factor authentication solutions, despite providing better security, may still be difficult for users to use if they are hard to handle, or require users to carry authenticators (tokens). These usability issues can lead to confusion and human error, reducing their effectiveness.

The majority of activities that people undertake are carried out in a fast and automatic mode, making people efficient but also making them vulnerable to security risks. It is unrealistic to expect people to always be cautious when they have numerous work emails with embedded links that may need to be clicked on. Productivity is threatened if they cannot complete their primary task without clicking on these links. Users must be educated as to the need for complex additional tasks and given options.

Factors such as fatigue, inexperience, and risk-taking attitude can lead to errors. Human factors such as memory limitations and shared assumptions also contribute. Factors such as time pressure, high workload, monotony, and boredom can lead to errors, as well as uncertainty about roles, responsibilities and rules. Work environment factors such as interruptions and poor equipment and lack of information can also cause errors, particularly when rules and procedures change. The responsibility to address these factors lies with the organization and regular reviews should be conducted to identify and address underlying causes of mistakes and near misses.

5.7. Security awareness education and training

Security awareness education helps people understand what the cybersecurity risks are and what they can do to reduce them. The emphasis is on why security matters, what it means for the organisation, and what it means for the individual. Education should be targeted and tailored to its audience, delivered in a way that is easy to understand and relevant. It should also be engaging, interactive and provide practical advice on how to reduce the risk.

Security training equips people with the skills that they need to reduce risk. Training should be focused on the tasks that people need to perform in order to be safe. It helps people acquire skills, such as how to use a security mechanism correctly or recognize and respond to a social engineering attack (e.g., a con artist). Training is more effective when it takes place in a social community and allows people to practice the skills and discuss their perceptions and biases. It should be practical, hands-on training that provides opportunities for people to practice what they have learned. It is also important that training be regularly reviewed and updated to keep pace with new risks and changing threats.

Simulations and games are often used to make security awareness more appealing and to support more comprehensive education and behavioral change. Anti-phishing simulations, which teach employees not to click on suspicious links in emails or elsewhere, are the most widely used in organizations. These simulations measure the impact of interventions and show a decrease in click rates in the short term. However, the success of these simulations depends on the employee's motivation to engage in the training and their ability to apply the skills being taught. Anti-phishing simulations can also have negative effects, such as reducing trust among employees or leading to reluctance to click on any links, including important ones. Designing simulations must take this issue into account. Using email filtering solutions can effectively reduce the number of suspicious emails.

Security education and training should be an integral part of an overall security strategy. They should be integrated with other security measures, such as technical controls and policies, to provide a comprehensive security solution. The key is to balance the need for security with the need for people to be able to complete their tasks efficiently and effectively.

5.8. Security policies

General MacArthur's statement to "never give an order that can't be obeyed" applies to security policies as well. When employees encounter security policies that are impossible or extremely difficult to follow or are clearly not effective, it undermines the credibility of all policies and the security professionals who issue them. If policies are not being followed, security professionals must investigate why this is the case and re-design the solution. In most cases, employees do not mean to show blatant disregard for security. They are usually trying to manage a risk that they understand in the best way they know how.

To make security a credible proposition, it must be framed as a positive aspect that enables people to engage in activities that they value and to experience positive outcomes. Key aspects of such "positive security" policy is to emphasize such positive outcomes and not blame those who are unable to follow security advice. This positive conception of security encourages individuals to become more involved in both decision-making and behaving securely.

> ## *"How would you like a job where, when you made a mistake, a big red light goes on and 18,000 people boo?"*
>
> – Jacques Plante, an ice hockey goaltender.

Protecting the Individual's Privacy

"My bank must stop trying to sell me identity theft protection. You know why I expect you to protect my money? Because you're a bank."

— Bill Maher, Comedian.

6.0. Introduction

In today's world, private individual's data are being collected, processed, and disseminated far and wide to persons unknown. The potential harms of such widespread use of private information due to a cybersecurity breach range from physical or psychological damage to individuals, to political and economic impacts.

There are systems that will protect users' privacy. The primary goals of privacy-preserving systems are to increase trust and minimize risk. These goals are achieved by disclosing as little as possible, collecting as little as possible, minimizing the replication and retention of data, cutting down on linkages between data, and avoiding centralization of data. Strategies such as these constrain the flow of information to parties other than those intended to receive it. Thus, the strategies limit the number of places where data is stored or processed, avoids a single point of potential fraudulent or adversarial attack, and limits the amount of time that the information is stored.

While still allowing information exchange, privacy technologies implement these strategies and preserve the integrity of the system. The first step in choosing a privacy technology is to identify the data flows that need to be minimized, and the minimum amount of information that needs to be transferred. Minimizing information flow includes keeping data within a firewall, encrypting the data, using cryptography, obfuscating, or anonymizing the data.

There are two main approaches to achieving data privacy. The first is data confidentiality (using confidentiality technologies) which focuses on preventing unauthorized access. This approach is typically achieved through the use of cryptography. The second approach is disclosure control (using control technologies) which involves both limiting the amount of information that is able to be leaked to the adversary, and ensuring, to the extent possible, that any leaked data cannot be linked to any specific individual.

"Don't trust people who tell you other people's secrets."

– Dan Howell, an English YouTube comedian.

6.1. Cryptography

Cryptography includes end-to-end encryption (E2EE) and Off-the-Record Messaging (OTR). E2EE protects the confidentiality of data in transit between the sender and recipient, while also ensuring integrity and authentication. In E2EE, the encryption keys are held by the devices at the end of the communication, which can be agreed upon using key transport or Diffie-Hellman exchange. This is a mathematical method of securely exchanging cryptographic keys over a public channel. OTR, on the other hand, strengthens privacy properties and considers an adversary who can observe and compromise the devices involved in communication.

As with most anything else, approaches such as cryptography come with trade-offs. They involve high resource requirements, and are characterized by low efficiency, and limited flexibility. There are alternative methods of obfuscating data that are less effective but more efficient. These methods control the amount of information that can be inferred from a data set. How well that works depends on the nature of the data and cleverness of the unintended receiver. The privacy gained from these techniques is based on limiting the available information, which may, of course, impact on its utility.

6.2. Anonymization

Anonymization is a technique used to process data without risking individual privacy. It separates identity from information by removing names or other identifiers. This makes the data unlinkable and lessens a reader's ability to make inferences about its meaning or importance. However, full anonymity is difficult to achieve as most data contain enough information to correlate different attributes and/or records in a database. Unique data patterns, called quasi-identifiers, can be used to re-identify individuals. To limit the risk of re-identification, anonymization is often combined with other obfuscation techniques such as generalization and suppression.

Generalization is a technique that reduces the precision of data by using ranges or statistics (such as an average), for example, instead of specific numbers.

Suppression is a technique that involves hiding part of the information. The idea is that the fewer data that are available, the more difficult it is to make inferences. For instance, instead of "Mary made a million dollars," the message instead states "One of the employees won an exceptional prize." The best privacy results can be obtained by using suppression strategies that are tailored to the nature and characteristics of the data but that can only be understood by a reader with prior knowledge of the topic at hand.

6.3. Metadata

Metadata are data about data. Examples are traffic metadata, device metadata, and location metadata.

Traffic metadata include information about the communication infrastructure such as identities of participants, data transfer amount and timing, and duration of connection. Metadata of this sort can be used to infer sensitive information about individuals or companies. Anonymous communication networks can protect against this risk. Such networks are formed by relays that change the appearance of messages through encryption and alter the traffic patterns.

Device metadata are associated with the platform generating the data and can, thus, reveal sensitive information about the device and its owner. To protect against this, various privacy-enhancing technologies such as Virtual Private Networks (VPNs), Tor, or encrypting device data can be used. Device metadata include specific characteristics of a user's device, such as browser type and version, screen resolution, installed fonts, that are often sent along with data requests in order to optimize the service provider's response. The information can be used to identify and track users, even if they are anonymous on the network layer. This process is called browser or device fingerprinting, which makes it possible for service providers to track users across the web. Defending against device metadata attacks is difficult, as hiding this information from online service providers affects device performance.

Location metadata are associated with the physical location from which data are generated. It reveals potentially sensitive information about an individual's location and activities. There are ways to protect against this by using a GPS spoofer or disabling location services on the devices that one uses.

6.4. Anonymous communications

The Tor network is the most popular anonymous communication network. It uses "onion" encryption to protect user's privacy by routing traffic through a series of Onion Routers (ORs). When a user wants to access a service, they install a Tor browser on their device. The browser builds a circuit of three ORs (entry, middle, and exit nodes) and routes encrypted traffic to the destination server through that circuit. A secret key is established with each of the ORs in the circuit and encrypts the packet in layers before it is sent to the destination server. The server sends data back in reverse order, i.e. the server encrypts the message in layers that are decrypted by exit, middle, and entry ORs. ORs do not purposely impose delays on messages, so that traffic patterns are conserved. This means that an attacker could link the origin and destination of communication by seeing both ends of the communication. Mix networks exist that protect against attacks by delaying messages or adding new real or dummy messages to the mix.

The difference between Tor and a VPN is that Tor is decentralized so that no single relay can learn the link between the sender and receiver. A VPN is centralized, meaning that a VPN provider can read the correspondence between the sender and receiver.

6.5. Control technologies

As opposed to simply keeping messages confidential, certain privacy technologies provide control over personal information. In many cases, revealing data may be necessary or perceived as beneficial, but it is important to consider the control over how the data is used. Privacy as control paradigm addresses concerns surrounding allowing users to express their preferences for data use, and also allowing organizations to define and enforce policies to prevent misuse of the data.

Complying with Cyber Law and Regulation

"When I was a kid, my mother told me I could be anyone I wanted to be.

Turns out, identity theft is a crime."

7.0. Introduction

Understanding "the law" helps business people know when to call in their lawyer, how to interpret the legal advice and how to value the lawyer's contributions. This chapter provides an introduction to business people of laws and regulations relevant to cybersecurity and privacy.

Legal risk management involves understanding the laws and regulations that apply in all the jurisdictions in which the business operates. It means the ability to assess the legal and enforcement risks that business can incur. Assessment is a challenging task due to the large number of laws and regulations, varying laws and enforcement authority across multiple jurisdictions, and the complexities of private law and regulatory systems.

Laws are created by the legislative authority, interpreted by the judicial authority, and enforced by the executive authority. Laws can be in the form of primary legislation, such as an Act of Congress, or secondary legislation where law-making authority is delegated to other regulatory agencies because of their technical expertise.

7.1. Civil law

Civil law governs private relationships between individuals. It deals with issues such as contracts, property rights, and torts (dealing with issues such as negligence). In contrast to criminal law, the focus of civil law is on compensation rather than punishment. Should a person breach a civil law that harms another person, the latter can sue. Civil law remedies include compensation, termination of a legal relationship, an injunction to stop harmful activities, or an order to take specific actions. In the context of cybersecurity, civil law deals with issues related to poor security practices in the development of information and communication technology products and services.

7.2. Criminal law

Criminal law governs behavior considered unacceptable by society. It is enforced by the state to deter bad behaviour, limit the ability of a criminal to cause harm, seek retribution for crime committed, compensate the victim, and (at least in theory) rehabilitate the criminal. The terms "guilty" and "innocent" are reserved for verdicts in criminal cases. Punishments include imprisonment, fines, forfeiture of criminal proceeds, and restitution to the victim.

7.3. Proof and evidence

The concept of "proof" in law refers to using permissible evidence to demonstrate the truth of events that are contested. Evidence can take various forms, such as witness testimony, business records, recordings, and photographs.

The standard of proof in law is the level of certainty required to demonstrate the truth of contested events. The standard varies depending on the type of legal matter, with criminal cases generally requiring a higher degree of certainty (beyond a reasonable doubt) compared to civil cases (balance of probabilities). The standard of proof must be met by the party carrying the burden of proof (generally the government in criminal matters or the person starting the legal proceedings in civil matters), who must use admissible evidence to prove their case to the finder of fact (e.g. judge, jury, or regulator).

Legal risk analysis often includes consideration of the rules and the relative ability of each party to prove their case. Therefore, documentation is necessary to prove one's case. Document retention policies are important to businesses. If a legal action is threatened, destruction of relevant evidence is illegal.

7.4. Jurisdiction

Jurisdiction refers to the authority of a state to assert legal power over entities operating within its literal and online territory. The principles of "conflict of laws" determines which law applies to resolve disputes that cross jurisdictional borders. The rise of online activities has led to an increase in cross-border legal responsibilities, making it important to consider jurisdiction and conflict of law principles.

There are three aspects of jurisdiction to consider: prescriptive jurisdiction, juridical jurisdiction, and enforcement jurisdiction. Prescriptive jurisdiction refers to the scope of a state's authority to make laws and regulate activities. Juridical jurisdiction refers to a court's authority to make decisions in a case. Enforcement jurisdiction refers to a state's ability to enforce its laws, including through arrest, or court order such as seizure of property. These concepts apply to multi-state activities conducted online.

States can claim prescriptive jurisdiction over non-resident persons who solicit business from residents or over actions taken by their own nationals while outside its borders. There may be cases where more than one state claims jurisdiction over a single act.

States assert prescriptive and juridical jurisdiction over actions that harm their residents, whether these actions take place within or outside of the state's territory. In the case of actions taking place outside of the state's territory, courts may interpret domestic law in a way that asserts jurisdiction if the content is visible to persons within the state. Examples of laws enforced in this manner include copyright, defamation, and gambling. This practice of asserting jurisdiction is based on the state's interest in protecting its residents and its domestic market.

States with computer crime laws often have jurisdiction over actions that target computers located within their territory, even if the person committing the action is located outside of the state. Cyberattackers who conduct offensive activity against computers located in another state are responsible if they violate the criminal law of that state, even if the activity is not illegal in the state where the cyberattacker is physically present.

The General Data Protection Regulation (GDPR) in the European Union (EU), brought a significant change to the territorial prescriptive jurisdiction of European data protection law. GDPR applies to the processing of personal data in the context of activities of a controller or processor (see the discussion of these terms and GDPR in the Data Protection section below) in the EU, regardless of where the processing takes place. GDPR asserts prescriptive jurisdiction over personal data processing activities anywhere in the world related to offering goods or services to, or monitoring the behaviour of, Europeans.

Police officers can arrest a person within their state's territory. An extradition order is required in order to arrest a criminal outside of the state. Extradition is governed by bilateral treaties and is only allowed if the crime is considered a crime in both states. The Budapest Convention, which mandates the inclusion of computer crimes in extradition procedures, serves as a legal basis for extradition between states without a bilateral treaty. Extradition requests for cybercrime suspects can sometimes be denied because there is no extradition treaty, the act was not criminal in both countries, or when there are concerns over treatment the accused will face.

States can order residents within their jurisdiction to produce data under their control, even if the data is stored outside the state's territory. States can also request mutual legal assistance from other states, but the process is often slow. Alternatives to this process include gathering evidence directly under the Budapest Convention which imposes requirements on states to provide mutual legal assistance and preserve electronic evidence in the investigation of cybercrime.

Technological intervention, such as content filtering, can be used by states or individuals to enforce laws or reduce the risk of legal consequences. States can enforce filtering by ordering it directly or by issuing orders to in-state internet service providers (ISPs) to block the receipt of offending content. Out-of-state entities that host offending content can also initiate filtering to limit transfers to states where it may result in liability.

Data sovereignty refers to a state's right to regulate and enforce jurisdiction over data stored within its territory. With the growth of cloud computing, the physical location of data storage has become less relevant, which has raised concerns about the number of states that might seek to enforce their jurisdiction over such data. Some states have responded to these concerns by mandating local storage and processing (localization) for certain types of data. The EU, for instance, has a localization requirement for personal data.

In rem jurisdiction (power over property) allows a state to assert control over property within its territory, and this power has been applied to seize and forfeit servers and domain names involved in illegal activities.

7.5. Privacy

Privacy law is about the legal right of a person to be free from intrusion by others into their personal affairs, also known as the "right to be left alone." In the context of cybersecurity, privacy law often arises in the context of electronic surveillance and related investigatory activity. This area of law is constantly evolving in response to new technologies and use cases, including those enabled by cloud data processing services.

The right to privacy is widely recognized as a human right, including for the reasons and examples set out the Democratic Values section of the Privacy chapter of this book. However, the right is not absolute and is subject to limitations and exceptions. The application of privacy principles to data, such as electronic communications, has evolved over time and is currently internationally accepted. The interpretation and implementation of privacy rights, however, varies among countries. Expectations of privacy can also vary between different societies and according to the nature of a person's relationship with the intruding party. As people rely on third-party cloud services for more personal aspects of their lives, privacy concerns over the data processed through these systems will lead to new legislation.

Metadata, the data that describe other data, is often treated differently from content data in privacy laws. Private information is disclosed through modern metadata such as URLs (website addresses), and location data from personal mobile data communications.

There is no harmonization of legal standards and procedures for lawful interception of online data. Service providers, such as communication companies, are usually subject to local laws that require them to provide facilities and technical assistance for lawful interception. As encryption becomes more widespread, states are facing difficulties accessing plaintext or unencrypted messages.

Providers of public communication services are usually restricted from intercepting communications that pass through their networks. Efforts to intercept communications on a third-party network is considered a crime under computer intrusion laws. Interception by a person on their own non-public network, such as on their LAN, may or may not be subject to computer crime legislation. In-house interception activities may be limited by privacy and data protection laws. Some privacy violations, such as unauthorized interceptions of communications or intrusion into data, can be prosecuted by the state as crimes.

7.6. Data protection

There are laws that govern how personal data is collected, processed, and stored. The laws are based on privacy principles, but they also address issues relevant to modern data processing techniques. The focus is on protecting individual rights to personal data. Data protection laws provide remedies for individuals whose privacy rights have been violated, such as the ability to seek monetary compensation through a legal action. Some violations of privacy, such as unauthorized interception of communications, are defined as crimes.

7.7. EU General Data Protection Regulation

The EU data protection law, referred to as GDPR, is meant to protect the privacy rights of individuals who are potentially identifiable through their communications. GDPR requires organizations to consider data protection from inception, and to implement measures that minimize the risk of data breaches. Implementation includes both technical and organizational measures that are appropriate for the risk level involved in the processing activity.

The definition of "personal data" under EU data protection law is broad and includes any information related to an identified or identifiable natural person. The definition covers not only obvious personal identifiers but also other factors that can lead to the identification of an individual. The term "personally identifiable information" or PII is often used in the US and may have different interpretations in different contexts, but it is not the same as "personal data".

EU data protection law has global impact through contract requirements imposed on non-EU data processors. It covers the processing of data – i.e. collection, recording, organization and storage. It also covers control of data, which means determining the purposes of the data and the methods by which it is processed.

There are principles for the lawful processing of personal data. They are: lawfulness, fairness, transparency, purpose limitation, data minimization, accuracy, storage limitation, integrity and confidentiality. Practitioners must be aware of sensitive personal data (e.g., racial origin, political opinions, and health data) which triggers additional protections and regulatory scrutiny. Consent for processing personal data is sometimes required and must be informed, clear, specific, and given freely.

The definitions of "processing" and "controller" and "processor" under GDPR make clear the roles and responsibilities of the two entities with respect to data. Processing is defined as any action taken with respect to personal data, including collection, recording, organization, and storage. The controller is the entity that determines the purposes and means of processing personal data, while the processor is the entity that carries out the processing on behalf of the controller.

Under law, controllers and processors must implement appropriate technical and organizational measures to ensure an appropriate level of security for processing personal data. Compliance requires appropriate technical measures as well as administrative management and oversight. GDPR provides examples of appropriate security measures, which include encryption. Security certifications help but are not considered guarantees of compliance with the law.

The transfer of personal data outside of the European Economic Area (EEA) is generally prohibited under GDPR. However, transfers can be made if the receiving country or international governmental organization has been found by the European Commission to have adequate legal protections in place. The process of obtaining an adequacy decision is initiated by the receiving state and often takes years of technical evaluation and diplomatic negotiation.

7.8. Data breach notification

The EU was first to impose requirements mandating the notification of personal data breaches to data subjects (individuals). The US has also started imposing a general duty to notify affected persons of personal data breaches. A personal data breach is defined as an accidental or unlawful destruction, loss, alteration, unauthorized disclosure of, or access to, personal data. The processor must first promptly notify the controller of the breach, and the controller must then notify the relevant supervisory authority, all within 72 hours. If the breach is likely to result in a high risk to the rights and freedoms of individuals, the controller must communicate the circumstances of the breach to these individuals. Communication to data subjects might, in some jurisdictions, be avoided if the controller has implemented measures to limit the harm caused by the breach, such as encryption because encryption reduces the potential harm that may come to data subjects.

GDPR carries significant legal risks for companies. This includes criminal prosecution, legal claims, enforcement notices, and large administrative fines. GDPR grants authority to impose fines of up to 4% of a company's annual worldwide turnover. Companies must assess and manage this risk at senior leadership levels and comply with all GDPR requirements.

7.9. Mandatory disclosure of incidents

Various jurisdictions have various legal requirements to disclose cybersecurity and privacy breaches to regulatory authorities in a timely manner. The rules vary based on jurisdiction and penalties for non-compliance can be onerous. Therefore, be sure to consult a lawyer.

In July 2023, for example, the US Securities and Exchange Commission (SEC) adopted rules requiring public companies to disclose material cybersecurity incidents that they experience and to disclose material information regarding their cybersecurity risk management, strategy, and governance.

The companies must disclose any cybersecurity incident they determine to be material and to describe the material aspects of the incident's nature, scope, and timing, as well as its material impact. *The disclosure is generally due four business days after the company determines that a cybersecurity incident is material.*

Companies must also disclosure their processes for assessing, identifying, and managing material risks from cybersecurity threats, as well as the material effects or reasonably likely material effects of risks from cybersecurity threats and previous cybersecurity incidents. The companies must disclose the board of directors' oversight of risks from cybersecurity threats and management's role and expertise in assessing and managing material risks from cybersecurity threats.

7.10. Crimes against information systems

Cybercrime generally refers to three categories of criminal activity: financial fraud using cyberspace, distribution of criminal content and hate speech over the internet, and crimes against cyberspace infrastructure such as computer system intrusion.

Early computer crime laws mainly focused on unauthorized intrusion into computer systems or improper modification of their contents. However, these laws became inadequate when DoS and DDoS (Denial of Service, e.g. overwhelming a computer system's processing power) attacks emerged. Currently, computer crime laws prohibit acts that cause a degradation in the performance of an information system, which includes Denial of Service.

Many legal systems prohibit the act of intercepting electronic communications without authorization, which is considered a violation of privacy. The penalties for this type of crime are often more severe if the communication is intercepted during its transmission on public networks. The production or distribution of tools with the intention of facilitating illegal activities against information systems is also considered a crime in many countries.

The penalties for committing a crime against information systems vary across countries and jurisdictions. Some people argue for longer sentences in cases where the acts cause significant damage to human welfare or national security.

7.11. Hacking back

The absence of a specific legal basis for "hacking back" (retaliation by a company against their presumed cyberattacker) has made the practice controversial. Many warn against "hacking back" due to the potential for significant harm (including retaliating against the wrong party and/or inducing more attacks) and the risk of prosecution. The deployment of any such countermeasures is likely to cause friction where different states are involved and may also pose risks to innocent third parties. As a result, the majority of states have rejected any notion of "self-help" in the context of cybersecurity, and instead maintain a preference for the use of state-led responses to cyberattacks, such as diplomatic and legal measures.

7.12. Contract law

A "contract" is a legally binding agreement between two or more parties. To be considered a contract, the agreement must show evidence of enforceability, such as consideration (value provided to each party) and intention to create a legal relationship. The specific time at which a contract is formed in online transactions can vary based on different legal systems but usually occurs once an offer has been transmitted and accepted.

Warranties are promises in contracts regarding the quality or legal status of goods or services, or the adequacy of information provided by one party. State contract laws usually add implied minimum warranties concerning the quality of goods and services. These include objective quality of goods, subjective quality of goods, and objective quality of services. Objective quality of goods refers to the promise that the goods delivered will be satisfactory to a normal buyer, while subjective quality of goods refers to the promise that the goods will meet the specific purpose of the buyer, who must disclose this purpose in advance. Objective quality of services refers to the promise that the service provider will exercise due care in delivering the service.

In the context of information and communications technology, it is common for vendors to attempt to exclude implied warranties, but it is more difficult to exclude in contracts with consumers. Limitations and exclusions of liability restrict financial responsibility for losses that may arise from the contracting relationship. An exclusion of liability seeks to avoid financial responsibility for certain types of financial loss, while a limitation of liability limits financial liability to a fixed sum or formula. These exclusions and limitations are often seen as a risk-reduction tool. However, they are viewed with suspicion by most contract law systems, especially when contracting with consumers.

In the event of a breach of contract, the non-breaching party has various remedies available, such as damages, recission, specific performance, and contractually mandated remedies. The severity of the breach often determines the type of remedy available. Damages are the most common remedy and aim to restore the financial expectation of the non-breaching party (i.e. putting the non-breaching party in the position they would have been without a breach). Recission is a more extreme remedy, used when the breach is severe, which declares the contract at an end and excuses the non-breaching party from further performance. Specific performance is also an extreme remedy and is reserved for situations where the breaching party is able take a simple action that satisfies the non-breaching party. Contractually mandated remedies, specified in the contract, can also be available but are often treated with suspicion by courts. Remedies are cumulative, meaning that a party can request multiple remedies for a single breach of contract.

7.13. Negligence

Negligence law (a part of "Tort" law) imposes a duty of care on a person to take reasonable steps to avoid causing harm to others. Negligence is a common basis of liability in many contexts, including cybersecurity, as individuals and organizations have a duty to take reasonable steps to protect against foreseeable harm. This duty includes taking steps to keep personal information secure and to prevent unauthorized access to confidential information. The victim must prove that the other party's conduct caused them harm. This obligation means that the victim must demonstrate that the harm would not have occurred but for the other party's conduct.

7.14. Liability

Product liability law is also relevant to cybersecurity. It imposes liability on manufacturers and sellers for harm caused by products that are not reasonably safe. This liability can arise from defects in the design, manufacturing, or labeling of the product, or from a failure to provide adequate warnings or instructions. In the context of cybersecurity, this can include liability for harm caused by defective software or hardware products, or for harm caused by a failure to provide adequate security measures.

Vicarious liability is a legal concept where an employer can be held responsible for the wrongful acts of their employees if those acts were committed within the scope of the employment relationship. Employers can avoid vicarious liability by insisting that employees act in lawful ways. This can be achieved through the development and enforcement of policies such as acceptable use policies, staff security standards, and employment policies.

Joint and several liability means that more than one party can be held responsible for causing harm to a single victim, and *any* of the responsible parties can be held liable for the *full* amount of damages awarded to the victim. This principle can become an issue when one of the defendants has limited financial resources or is located in a foreign jurisdiction where it is difficult to enforce a judgment. Companies should be mindful of this principle when working with partners or collaborators who may not have the financial resources to cover their share of a damages award in the event of a data protection violation.

7.15. Be aware

The laws and regulations of each jurisdiction where a business operates will significantly affect business operations. The need to understand and comply with local data protection, privacy, and security laws is important for businesses operating online. All businesses need to be aware of the extra-territorial reach of certain laws and regulations.

Cybersecurity practitioners need to be aware of the risks not only to their employer, but, should they ever be tempted or instructed to break criminal law, also to their own personal reputation, safety and liberty. Practitioners may personally face consequences for their actions, regardless of whatever incentives may have been provided to them by their employer.

Seeking the advice of experienced legal counsel will help to mitigate legal risk. This chapter provides information about legal principles and examples of laws and regulations. It is not legal advice. For legal advice, please consult a lawyer.

Conclusion

"Security in IT is like locking your house or car – it doesn't stop the bad guys, but if it's good enough they may move on to an easier target."

Paul Herbka, Cybersecurity professional

This book, a non-technical introduction to the practice of cybersecurity, has introduced the challenges of protection of information systems and also the methods by which these challenges can be met.

Every organization is different and will have different issues and priorities. Furthermore, cybersecurity is continually evolving. Therefore, organizations must hire professional cybersecurity experts and listen to and follow their advice.

While this book should not be relied on for implementation of cybersecurity, readers should now better understand why to hire cybersecurity professionals, what those professionals are recommending, and what questions to ask them.

*"By encrypting all our data, the hackers can't read it,
our unauthorized personnel can't read it,
and, I'm afraid, neither can we."*

*"Dictionaries are like watches;
the worst is better than none,
and the best cannot be expected
to go quite true."*

– Samuel Johnson

The Cybersecurity Dictionary

A

2FA: Two factor authentication.

AAL: Authentication assurance level.

Access: To make contact with one or more functions of an online, digital service.

Access control mechanism: Security measures designed to detect and deny unauthorized access and permit authorized access to an information system or a physical facility.

Access control: The process of granting or denying specific requests for or attempts to: obtain and use information and related information processing services; and enter specific physical facilities.

Access: The ability and means to communicate with or otherwise interact with a system, to use system resources to handle information, to gain knowledge of the information the system contains, or to control system components and functions.

Access point: A device that enables wireless devices to connect to a wired network.

Accidental insider: An employee who accidentally introduces cybersecurity risk due to poor cybersecurity practices, such as accidentally click on a suspicious phishing link.

Actions: Using command and control of the installed ransomware to copy, destroy, or alter data, either immediately or in the future.

Active attack: An actual assault perpetrated by an intentional threat source that attempts to alter a system, its resources, its data, or its operations.

Active content: Software that is able to automatically carry out or trigger actions without the explicit intervention of a user.

Activation: The process of inputting an activation factor into a multi-factor authenticator to enable its use for authentication.

Active attack: An attack on the authentication protocol where the attacker transmits data to the claimant, Credential Service Provider (CSP), verifier, or Relying Party (RP). Examples of active attacks include man-in-the-middle, impersonation, and session hijacking.

Administrative privileges: Permissions that allow a computer user to perform certain functions on a system, such as installing software and changing configuration settings.

Administrator: A person who administers a computer system or network and has access to the administrator account which has wide, sometimes complete, access to all data on the system, i.e. an "all-access" pass.

Advanced persistent threat: A long-term stealth cyberattack. Also a group, such as a state actor, with advanced cyberattack capabilities.

Advanced persistent threat: An adversary that possesses sophisticated levels of expertise and significant resources which allow it to create opportunities to achieve its objectives by using multiple attack vectors (e.g., cyber, physical, and deception).

Adversary: An individual, group, organization, or government that conducts or has the intent to conduct detrimental activities.

Air gap: To physically separate or isolate a system from other systems or networks.

Alert: A notification that a specific attack has been detected or directed at an organization's information systems.

All source intelligence: Analyzing threat information from multiple sources, disciplines, and agencies. Synthesizing and placing intelligence information in context; drawing insights about the possible implications.

Allowlist: A list of entities that are considered trustworthy and are granted access or privileges.

Analyze: Highly specialized reviewing and evaluation of incoming cybersecurity information to determine its usefulness for intelligence.

Antispyware software: A program that specializes in detecting and blocking or removing forms of spyware.

Antivirus software: A program that monitors a computer or network to detect or identify major types of malicious code and to prevent or contain malware incidents. Sometimes by removing or neutralizing the malicious code.

Antivirus: Software used to prevent, detect, and remove malware.

API: Application Programming Interface.

Applicant: A subject undergoing the processes of enrollment and identity proofing.

Application: Software installed on a system.

Application programming interface: A set of protocols and standards that allow different software applications to communicate with each other.

Application security: The process of designing, testing, and implementing security measures to protect software applications from unauthorized access, modification, or destruction.

Approved cryptography: Federal Information Processing Standard (FIPS)-approved or NIST recommended. An algorithm or technique that is either 1) specified in a FIPS or NIST Recommendation, or 2) adopted in a FIPS or NIST Recommendation.

APT: Advanced persistent threat.

Assertion: A statement from a verifier to an RP that contains information about a subscriber.

Assertion reference: A data object, created in conjunction with an assertion, that identifies the verifier and includes a pointer to the full assertion held by the verifier.

Asset: A person, structure, facility, information, and records, information technology systems and resources, material, process, relationships, or reputation that has value.

Asymmetric cryptography: Public key cryptography.

Asymmetric keys: Two related keys, comprised of a public key and a private key, that are used to perform complementary operations such as encryption and decryption or signature verification and generation.

Attack method: The manner or technique and means an adversary may use in an assault on information or an information system.

Attack mode: Attack method.

Attack path: The steps that an adversary takes or may take to plan, prepare for, and execute an attack.

Attack pattern: Similar cyber events or behaviors that may indicate an attack has occurred or is occurring, resulting in a security violation or a potential security violation.

Attack signature: A characteristic or distinctive pattern that can be searched for or that can be used in matching to previously identified attacks.

Attack surface: The set of ways in which an adversary can enter a system and potentially cause damage. An information system's characteristics that permit an adversary to probe, attack, or maintain presence in the information system.

Attack vector: Attack method.

Attack: An attempt to gain unauthorized access to system services, resources, or information, or an attempt to compromise system integrity.

Attacker: An individual, group, organization, or government that executes an attack. A party acting with malicious intent to compromise an information system.

Attacker-in-the-middle attack: Man-in-the-middle attack.

Attribute: A quality or characteristic ascribed to someone or something.

Attribute value: A complete statement asserting a property of a subscriber, independent of format. For example, for the attribute birthday, a value could be 12/1/1980 or December 1, 1980.

Audit Trail: A record of events that allows administrators to trace and examine activities and changes on a system or network.

Authentication: The process of verifying the identity or other attributes of an entity (user, process, or device). The process of verifying the source and integrity of data.

Authentication factor: The three types of authentication factors are something you know, something you have, and something you are. Every authenticator has one or more authentication factors.

Authentication intent: The process of confirming the claimant's intent to authenticate or reauthenticate by including a process requiring user intervention in the authentication flow. Some authenticators (e.g., OTP devices) establish authentication intent as part of their operation, others require a specific step, such as pressing a button, to establish intent. Authentication intent is a countermeasure against use by malware of the endpoint as a proxy for authenticating an attacker without the subscriber's knowledge.

Authentication protocol: A defined sequence of messages between a claimant and a verifier that demonstrates that the claimant has possession and control of one or more valid authenticators to establish their identity, and, optionally, demonstrates that the claimant is communicating with the intended verifier.

Authentication secret: A generic term for any secret value that an attacker could use to impersonate the subscriber in an authentication protocol. These are further divided into short-term authentication secrets, which are only useful to an attacker for a limited period of time, and long-term authentication secrets, which allow an attacker to impersonate the subscriber until they are manually reset. The authenticator secret is the canonical example of a long-term authentication secret, while the authenticator output, if it is different from the authenticator secret, is usually a short-term authentication secret.

Authenticator: Token. Something the claimant possesses and controls (typically a cryptographic module or password) that is used to authenticate the claimant's identity.

Authentication assurance level: A category describing the strength of the authentication process.

Authenticator output: The output value generated by an authenticator. The ability to generate valid authenticator outputs on demand proves that the claimant possesses and controls the authenticator. Protocol messages sent to the verifier are dependent upon the authenticator output, but they may or may not explicitly contain it.

Authenticator secret: The secret value contained within an authenticator.

Authenticator type: A category of authenticators with common characteristics. Some authenticator types provide one authentication factor, others provide two.

Authenticity: A property achieved through cryptographic methods of being genuine and being able to be verified and trusted, resulting in confidence in the validity of a transmission, information or a message, or sender of information or a message.

Authoritative source: An entity that has access to, or verified copies of, accurate information from an issuing source such that a CSP can confirm the validity of the identity evidence supplied by an applicant during identity proofing. An issuing source may also be an authoritative source. Often, authoritative sources are determined by a policy decision of the agency or CSP before they can be used in the identity proofing validation phase.

Authorization: A process of determining, by evaluating applicable access control information, whether a subject is allowed to have the specified types of access to a particular resource. The process or act of granting access privileges or the access privileges as granted.

AV: Antivirus.

Availability: Ensuring timely and reliable access to and use of information and preventing disruption in information access.

B

Backdoor: An undocumented, private, or less-detectible method of gaining remote access to a computer, bypassing authentication measures.

Backup: A copy of files, data and software made to facilitate recovery of a system.

Bearer assertion: The assertion a party presents as proof of identity, where possession of the assertion itself is sufficient proof of identity for the assertion bearer.

BEC: Business Email Compromise.

Binding: An association between a subscriber identity and an authenticator or given subscriber session.

Biometric reference: One or more stored biometric samples, templates, or models attributed to an individual and used as the object of biometric comparison. For example, a facial image stored digitally on a passport, fingerprint minutiae template on a National ID card or Gaussian Mixture Model for speaker recognition in a database.

Biometric sample: An analog or digital representation of biometric characteristics prior to biometric feature extraction. An example is a record containing a fingerprint image.

Biometrics: Automated recognition of individuals based on their biological and behavioral characteristics.

BIA: Business impact analysis.

Black hat: Criminals who seek to access systems to exploit vulnerabilities for cybercrime.

Blocklist: A list of entities that are blocked or denied privileges or access.

Blue team: A group that defends an organization's information systems when mock attackers (i.e., the Red Team) attack, typically as part of an operational exercise conducted according to rules established and monitored by a neutral group (i.e., the White Team). Also, a group that conducts operational vulnerability evaluations and recommends mitigation techniques to customers who need an independent technical review of their cybersecurity posture.

Bot master: The controller of a botnet that, from a remote location, provides direction to the compromised computers in the botnet.

Bot: A computer connected to the Internet that has been surreptitiously or secretly compromised with malicious logic to perform activities under remote the command and control of a remote administrator. A member of a larger collection of compromised computers known as a botnet.

Botnet: A network of hijacked computers and devices infected with malware and remotely controlled by a cyberattacker.

Browser fingerprinting: A technique used to track or identify users based on the unique characteristics of their web browser, such as installed fonts, language, plug-ins, or screen resolution.

Browser hijacking: A type of cyberattack that takes control of a user's web browser, often redirecting the user to malicious websites or installing unwanted software.

Browser isolation: A security technique that isolates web browsers from the underlying operating system and network, typically using virtualization or sandboxing, to prevent web-based cyberattacks.

Brute force attack: Automatic entry of millions of combinations of characters in repetitive login attempts until the cyberattacker successfully obtains a password.

Buffer overflow: A type of cyberattack that exploits vulnerabilities in software applications to overflow a buffer or memory space, typically causing the application to crash or execute malicious code.

Bug bounty program: A program that rewards individuals or security researchers for identifying and reporting security vulnerabilities or weaknesses in software applications or systems.

Bug fix patch: Repairs functionality issues in software.

Bug: An unexpected and relatively small defect, fault, flaw, or imperfection in an information system or device.

Build security in: A set of principles, practices, and tools to design, develop, and evolve information systems and software that enhance resistance to vulnerabilities, flaws, and attacks.

Business continuity planning: Disaster recovery planning.

Business email compromise: A type of cyberattack that uses social engineering and phishing techniques to impersonate an executive or employee in a company and fraudulently obtain money or sensitive information.

Business impact analysis: Predicts how disruptions or incidents will harm an organization's operations, business processes, systems, and finances.

108

C

Capability: The means to accomplish a mission, function, or objective.

CAPTCHA: Completely Automated Public Turing test to tell Computers and Humans Apart. An interactive feature added to web forms to distinguish whether a human or automated agent is using the form. Typically, it requires entering text corresponding to a distorted image or a sound stream.

Certificate authority: A trusted third-party organization that issues and manages digital certificates, often used for secure authentication, encryption, and identification in online transactions.

Challenge-response protocol: An authentication protocol where the verifier sends the claimant a challenge (usually a random value or nonce) that the claimant combines with a secret (such as by hashing the challenge and a shared secret together, or by applying a private key operation to the challenge) to generate a response that is sent to the verifier. The verifier can independently verify the response generated by the claimant (such as by re-computing the hash of the challenge and the shared secret and comparing to the response, or performing a public key operation on the response) and establish that the claimant possesses and controls the secret.

Chief Information Officer/Chief Information Security Officer: Person responsible for ensuring the security of systems and data in an organization.

CIO/CISO: Chief Information Officer/Chief Information Security Officer.

Cipher: Cryptographic algorithm.

Ciphertext: Data or information in its encrypted form.

CIRT: Cyber incident response team.

Claimant: A subject whose identity is to be verified using one or more authentication protocols.

Claimed identity: An applicant's declaration of unvalidated and unverified personal attributes.

Cloud computing: The use of remote servers hosted on the internet. Cloud computing allows users to access a shared pool of computing resources, including networks, servers, applications, or services, on demand and from anywhere.

Cloud service provider: A company that provides cloud computing services, e.g. Amazon AWS.

Code injection: A type of attack that exploits vulnerabilities in applications to inject malicious code or scripts into a target system, often used for privilege escalation, data theft, or remote control.

Collect and operate: Specialized denial and deception operations and collection of cybersecurity information that may be used to develop intelligence.

Collection operations: Executing collection using appropriate strategies and within the priorities established through the collection management process.

Command and control: A computer on the internet used by the cyberattacker to send commands to systems compromised by ransomware and to receive stolen data.

Common vulnerabilities and exposures: A collection of publicly known cybersecurity vulnerabilities and exposures, often used to identify and prioritize vulnerabilities for remediation or mitigation.

Computer forensics: Digital forensics.

Computer network defense analysis: Using defensive measures and information collected from a variety of sources to identify, analyze, and report events that occur or might occur within the network in order to protect information, information systems, and networks from threats.

Computer network defense infrastructure support: Testing, implementing, deploying, maintaining, reviewing, and administering the infrastructure hardware and software that are required to effectively manage the computer network defense service provider network and resources; monitors network to actively remediate unauthorized activities.

Computer network defense: The actions taken to defend against unauthorized activity within computer networks.

Computer security incident: Event or incident.

Confidentiality: The prevention of damage to, protection of, and restoration of computers, electronic communications systems, electronic communications services, wire communication, and electronic communication, including information, to ensure its availability, integrity, authentication, confidentiality, and nonrepudiation.

Consequence: The effect of an event, incident, or occurrence. The effect of a loss of confidentiality, integrity or availability of information or an information system on an organization's operations, its assets, on individuals, other organizations, or on national interests.

Contingency planning: Disaster recovery planning.

Continuity of operations plan: A document that sets forth procedures for the continued performance of core capabilities and critical operations during any disruption or potential disruption.

Cookies: Small text files that are stored on a user's computer when they visit a website. They are often used to track user behavior and preferences, and can be used for targeted advertising.

Core attributes: The set of identity attributes the CSP has determined and documented to be required for identity proofing.

Credential: An object or data structure that authoritatively binds an identity – via an identifier or identifiers – and (optionally) additional attributes, to at least one authenticator possessed and controlled by a subscriber. A credential is issued, stored, and maintained by the CSP. Copies of information from the credential can be possessed by the subscriber, typically in the form of a one or more digital certificates that are often contained, along with their associated private keys, in an authenticator.

Credential service provider: A trusted entity whose functions include identity proofing applicants to the identity service and the registration of authenticators to subscriber accounts. A CSP may be an independent third party.

Credential stuffing: A type of cyberattack that uses stolen or leaked login credentials to gain unauthorized access to other accounts or services, often through automated scripts or tools.

Criminal: A person who has committed or is committing a crime contrary to a state's criminal law. Criminal law is enforced by the state to deter bad behaviour, limit the ability of a criminal to cause harm, seek retribution for crime committed, compensate the victim, and (at least in theory) rehabilitate the criminal. Punishments include imprisonment, fines, forfeiture of criminal proceeds, and restitution to the victim.

Critical infrastructure and key resources: Critical infrastructure.

Critical infrastructure: Physical and virtual assets that are essential to the operation of an organization or a state.

Cross-site request forgery: An attack in which a subscriber currently authenticated to an RP and connected through a secure session browses to an attacker's website, causing the subscriber to unknowingly invoke unwanted actions at the RP. For example, if a bank website is vulnerable to a CSRF attack, it may be possible for a subscriber to unintentionally authorize a large money transfer, merely by viewing a malicious link in a webmail message while a connection to the bank is open in another browser window.

Cross-site scripting: A vulnerability that allows attackers to inject malicious code into an otherwise benign website. These scripts acquire the permissions of scripts generated by the target website and can therefore compromise the confidentiality and integrity of data transfers between the website and client. Websites are vulnerable if they display user-supplied data from requests or forms without sanitizing the data so that it is not executable.

Cryptanalysis: The operations performed in defeating or circumventing cryptographic protection of information by applying mathematical techniques and without an initial knowledge of the key employed in providing the protection. The study of mathematical techniques for attempting to defeat or circumvent cryptographic techniques and/or information systems security.

Cryptocurrency: Tradable electronic tokens such as bitcoin.

Cryptographic algorithm: A well-defined computational procedure that takes variable inputs, including a cryptographic key, and produces an output.

Cryptographic authenticator: An authenticator that proves possession of an authentication secret through direct communication, via the endpoint, with a verifier.

Cryptographic key: A value used to control cryptographic operations, such as decryption, encryption, signature generation, or signature verification.

Cryptographic module: A set of hardware, software, and/or firmware that implements approved security functions (including cryptographic algorithms and key generation).

Cryptography: The use of mathematical techniques to provide security services, such as confidentiality, data integrity, entity authentication, and data origin authentication. The art or science concerning the principles, means, and methods for converting plaintext into ciphertext and for restoring encrypted ciphertext to plaintext.

Cryptology: The mathematical science that deals with cryptanalysis and cryptography.

CSP: Cloud service provider (in computing) or Credential service provider (in digital identity).

CSRF: Cross-site request forgery.

Customer service and technical support: Addressing problems, installing, configuring, troubleshooting, and providing maintenance and training in response to customer requirements or inquiries (e.g., tiered-level customer support).

CVE: Common Vulnerabilities and Exposures.

Cyber ecosystem: The interconnected information infrastructure of interactions among persons, processes, data, and information and communications technologies, along with the environment and conditions that influence those interactions.

Cyber exercise: A planned event during which an organization simulates a cyber disruption to develop or test capabilities such as preventing, detecting, mitigating, responding to or recovering from the disruption.

Cyber hygiene: The basic practices and habits used to maintain good cybersecurity hygiene and protect against common threats, such as strong passwords, software updates, and backups.

Cyber incident response plan: Incident response plan.

Cyber incident response team: An internal team for incident response.

Cyber incident: Event or incident.

Cyber infrastructure: An electronic information and communications systems and services and the information contained therein. The information and communications systems and services composed of all hardware and software that process, store, and communicate information, or any combination of all of these elements: Processing includes the creation, access, modification, and destruction of information. Storage includes paper, magnetic, electronic, and all other media types. Communications include sharing and distribution of information.

Cyber insurance: A type of insurance policy that provides coverage for losses or damages related to cyberattacks, data breaches, and other cybersecurity incidents.

Cyber kill chain: A series of steps that trace the stages of a cyberattack from the cyberattacker's early reconnaissance stages to the cyberattacker's exfiltration of data. Reconnaissance: the observation stage; cyberattackers assess from the outside to identify targets and tactics. Intrusion: access into the systems, often leveraging malware or security vulnerabilities. Exploitation: taking advantage of vulnerabilities, and delivering malicious code. Privilege escalation: cyberattackers often need more privileges to get access to more data. Therefore, once inside a system, they use techniques to increase their own access privileges, often to the most powerful "administrator" status.

Cyber operations planning: Performing in-depth joint targeting and cyber planning process. Gathering information and develops detailed Operational Plans and Orders supporting requirements. Conducting strategic and operational-level planning across the full range of operations for integrated information and cyberspace operations.

Cyber operations: Performing activities to gather evidence on criminal or foreign intelligence entities in order to mitigate possible or real-time threats, protecting against espionage or insider threats, foreign sabotage, international terrorist activities, or supporting other intelligence activities.

Cyber range: A virtual or physical environment used for cybersecurity training, testing, or simulation, often including real-world scenarios and exercises to improve skills and readiness.

Cyberattack: Information security event caused by a attacker.

Cyberattacker: Attacker.

Cybercrime: Technology-enabled crimes, generally for personal or financial gain.

Cybercriminal: Attacker.

Cyberespionage: The practice of theft of confidential information for the purposes of covert, unethical and/or illegal competition among individuals, organizations or nations.

Cybersecurity: People, processes, and technologies which prevent damage to, protect, and restore computers, electronic communications systems and services, and information to ensure information confidentiality, integrity, and availability.

Cybersecurity culture: The values, beliefs, and behaviors that shape an organization's approach to cybersecurity, often including leadership commitment, employee awareness and training, and shared responsibility for security.

D

Data administration: Developing and administering databases and/or data management systems that allow for the storage, query, and utilization of data.

Data aggregation: The process of gathering and combining data from different sources, so that the combined data reveals new information. The new information is more sensitive than the individual data elements themselves and the person who aggregates the data was not granted access to the totality of the information.

Data breach: The unauthorized movement or disclosure of sensitive information to a party, usually outside the organization, that is not authorized to have or see the information.

Data classification: The process of categorizing data based on its sensitivity or importance to an organization, often used to determine appropriate security controls and handling procedures.

Data integrity: The property that data is complete, intact, and trusted and has not been modified or destroyed in an unauthorized or accidental manner.

Data leakage: Data breach.

Data loss prevention: A set of procedures and mechanisms to stop sensitive data from leaving a security boundary.

Data loss: The result of unintentionally or accidentally deleting data, forgetting where it is stored, or exposure to an unauthorized party.

Data masking: A technique used to hide or obscure sensitive or confidential data by replacing or obscuring the original data with a substitute, often used to protect data privacy and security.

Data mining: The process or techniques used to analyze large sets of existing information to discover previously unrevealed patterns or correlations.

Data spill: Data breach.

Data theft: The deliberate or intentional act of stealing of information.

Data: A representation of facts, concepts, or instructions.

Database: An organized collection of data stored and accessed electronically.

Deception: The practice of using decoys, honeypots, or other techniques to mislead or divert cyber attackers and enhance situational awareness and response.

Decipher: To convert enciphered text to plain text by means of a cryptographic system.

Decode: To convert encoded text to plain text by means of a code.

Decrypt: A generic term encompassing decode and decipher.

Decryption: The process of transforming ciphertext into its original plaintext. The process of converting encrypted data back into its original form.

Deep packet inspection: A technique used to inspect and analyze network traffic at the packet level to detect and prevent security threats, often used by firewalls, intrusion detection and prevention systems, and network analytics tools.

Defence-in-depth: A cybersecurity concept in which multiple layers of security are used to protect the integrity of information. These layers can include antivirus software, firewalls, hierarchical passwords, intrusion detection, and biometric identification.

Delivery: Distribution of the ransomware to the target system, e.g. by an email phishing attachment.

Denial of service: A cyberattack that successfully prevents or impairs the normal functioning of systems by using all of its capacity. Such an attack commonly uses thousands of devices accessing a website simultaneously and continually, leading to overload and inability to deliver webpages to legitimate users.

Derived attribute value: A statement asserting a property of a subscriber without necessarily containing identity information, independent of format. For example, instead of requesting the attribute birthday, a derived value could be older than 18. Instead of requesting the attribute for physical address, a derived value could be currently residing in this district.

Designed-in security: Build security in.

Detect: Develop and implement the appropriate activities to identify the occurrence of a cyberattack.

Devices: System equipment, including computers, servers, printers and telephones.

Differential backup: Incremental backup.

Digital authentication: The process of establishing confidence in user identities presented digitally to a system.

Digital certificate: A type of electronic document that verifies the identity of the owner of a public key, often used to secure online transactions and communications.

Digital forensics: The processes and specialized techniques for gathering, retaining, and analyzing system-related data, i.e. digital evidence, for investigative purposes. Collecting, processing, preserving, analyzing, and presenting computer-related evidence in support of network vulnerability, mitigation, and/or criminal, fraud, counterintelligence or law enforcement investigations.

Digital rights management: A form of access control technology to protect and manage use of digital content or devices in accordance with the content or device provider's intentions.

Digital signature: A value computed with a cryptographic process using a private key and then appended to a data object, thereby digitally signing the data. Digital signatures provide authenticity protection, integrity protection, and non-repudiation, but not confidentiality protection.

Disaster recovery planning: How to resume normal operations after a cyberattack.

Disruption: An event which causes unplanned interruption in operations or functions for an unacceptable length of time.

Distributed denial of service: A denial of service technique that uses numerous systems to perform the attack simultaneously. Denial of service.

DMARC: Domain-based message authentication, reporting and conformance.

DNS: Domain name system.

DNS spoofing: A type of cyber attack that involves redirecting or manipulating the Domain Name System (DNS) to redirect users to fake or malicious websites or to intercept communications.

Domain name system: The "telephone book" for the internet used for both human-initiated actions such as visiting a website and machine-initiated actions such as running an update. It translates destinations such as "gmail.com" into a specific computer number such as "8.8.8.8" that a computer can understand.

Domain-based message authentication, reporting and conformance: Allows senders and receivers of email to improve and monitor protection of the domain name being used for fraudulent email.

DoS: Denial of service.

Double extortion schemes: Ransomware cyberattackers steal sensitive data from the organization and encrypt the system files and demand ransom. However, with double extortion, even if the ransom is paid and the system files are decrypted, the cyberattackers then threaten to publish or sell the stolen data unless the victim pays a second ransom.

DPI: Deep Packet Inspection.

Drive-by download: When a user unknowingly visits a malicious website where malware is surreptitiously automatically downloaded and installed.

Dumpster diving: A type of physical security breach that involves rummaging through an organization's garbage or recycling bins to find sensitive or confidential information, often used for identity theft or fraud.

Dynamic attack surface: The automated, on-the-fly changes of an information system's characteristics to thwart actions of an adversary.

E

Eavesdropping attack: An attack in which an attacker listens passively to the authentication protocol to capture information that can be used in a subsequent active attack to masquerade as the claimant.

EDR: Endpoint Detection and Response.

Education and training: Conducting training of personnel within pertinent subject domain; developing, planning, coordinating, delivering, and/or evaluating training courses, methods, and techniques as appropriate.

Electronic signature: Any mark in electronic form associated with an electronic document, applied with the intent to sign the document.

Email spoofing: A type of cyberattack that involves falsifying the sender's email address to appear as if it came from a trusted source, often used for phishing, spamming, or social engineering attacks.

Encipher: To convert plaintext to ciphertext by means of a cryptographic system.

Encode: To convert plaintext to ciphertext by means of a code.

Encrypt: The generic term encompassing encipher and encode.

Encryption: A process of making electronically stored information unreadable to anyone not having the correct password or key. The process uses cryptography to convert plain (readable) text into cipher (unreadable) text to prevent anyone except the intended recipient from reading the data.

Encryption: The process of transforming plaintext into ciphertext. Converting data into a form that cannot be easily understood by unauthorized people.

Endpoint detection and response: A security technology that monitors and detects suspicious activity on endpoints (devices such as laptops, mobile phones, or servers), such as malware infections, network anomalies, or unauthorized access, and responds with automated or manual actions to prevent or mitigate the impact of a cyber attack (including antivirus software, firewalls, and intrusion detection systems). Also, referred to as endpoint security.

Enrollment: The process through which an applicant applies to become a subscriber of a CSP and the CSP validates the applicant's identity.

Enterprise risk management: A comprehensive approach to risk management that engages people, processes, and systems across an organization to improve the quality of decision making for managing risks that may hinder an organization's ability to achieve its objectives. Involves identifying mission dependencies on enterprise capabilities, identifying and prioritizing risks due to defined threats, implementing countermeasures to provide both a static risk posture and an effective dynamic response to active threats; and assessing enterprise performance against threats and adjusts countermeasures as necessary.

Entropy: A measure of the amount of uncertainty an attacker faces to determine the value of a secret. Entropy is usually stated in bits. A value having n bits of entropy has the same degree of uncertainty as a uniformly distributed n-bit random value.

Event: An observable occurrence in an information system or network. Sometimes provides an indication that an incident is occurring or at least raise the suspicion that an incident may be occurring.

Exfiltrate: Stealing and removing data from a compromised system. The unauthorized transfer of information from an information system.

Exploit: A technique to breach the security of a network or information system in violation of security policy.

Exploitation analysis: Analyzing collected information to identify vulnerabilities and potential for exploitation.

Exploitation: Taking advantage of cybersecurity vulnerabilities, and delivering malware into a system.

Exposure: The condition of being unprotected, thereby allowing access to information or access to capabilities that an attacker can use to enter a system or network.

F

Failure: The inability of a system or component to perform its required functions within specified performance requirements.

False positive: A security alert or warning that is triggered by legitimate activity or behavior, rather than by a genuine security threat or attack.

Feature patch: Adds new functions to the software.

Federation: A process that allows the conveyance of identity and authentication information across a set of networked systems.

Federation protocol and identity provider: An identity provider for a Federation process.

FIDO: A set of open standards for authentication, using strong multi-factor authentication methods such as biometrics or hardware tokens, to improve security and reduce reliance on passwords.

Firewall: A security barrier placed between two networks that controls the amount and type of network traffic that may pass between the two. The barrier protects local system resources from being accessed from the outside.

Forensics: Digital forensics.

G

Gateway: A device or software program that connects two networks or systems, often used to control and filter traffic, provide security, and enable communication between different types of networks.

H

Hacker: An unauthorized user, Black hat or White hat, who attempts to or gains access to an information system.

Hacktivist: Politically or ideologically motivated threat agent who aims to damage the organization.

Hash value: A numeric value resulting from applying a mathematical algorithm against a set of data such as a file.

Hashing: A process of applying a mathematical algorithm against a set of data to produce a numeric value (a "hash value") that represents the data. Mapping a bit string of arbitrary length to a fixed length bit string to produce the hash value.

Hazard: A natural or man-made source or cause of harm or difficulty.

Honeypot: A decoy system or network used to detect, deflect, or counteract cyber attacks by attracting and analyzing attacker behavior or malware.

I

IAL: Identity assurance Level.

ICT supply chain threat: A man-made threat achieved through exploitation of the information and communications technology (ICT) system's supply chain, including acquisition processes.

ICT: Information and communications technology.

Identify: Develop the organizational understanding to manage cybersecurity risk to systems, assets, data, and capabilities.

Identity and access management: The methods and processes used to manage subjects and their authentication and authorizations to access specific objects.

Identity assurance level: A category that conveys the degree of confidence that the applicant's claimed identity is their real identity.

Identity: Details describing who a person is on a system, e.g. their username. An attribute or set of attributes that uniquely describe a subject within a given context.

Identity evidence: Information or documentation provided by the applicant to support the claimed identity. Identity evidence may be physical (e.g. a driver license) or digital (e.g. an assertion generated and issued by a CSP based on the applicant successfully authenticating to the CSP).

Identity proofing: The process by which a CSP collects, validates, and verifies information about a person.

Identity resolution: The process of collecting information about an applicant in order to uniquely distinguish an individual within the context of the population the CSP serves.

IdP: Federation protocol and identity provider.

IDPS: Intrusion detection / prevention system.

IDS: Intrusion detection system.

Impact: The effect on organizational operations, organizational assets, individuals, other organizations, or national security interests of a loss of confidentiality, integrity, or availability of information or a system. Consequence.

Improper usage: A user violates the organization's acceptable computing-use policies.

Incident management: The management and coordination of activities associated with an actual or potential occurrence of an event that may result in adverse consequences to information or information systems.

Incident response plan: A set of predetermined and documented procedures to detect and respond to a cyber incident.

Incident response: Assess, document, and respond to incidents, restore an organization's systems, recover information, and reduce the risk of the cyberattack reoccurring.

Incident: An occurrence that actually or potentially results in adverse consequences to an information system or the information that the system processes, stores, or transmits and that may require a response action to mitigate the consequences. An occurrence that constitutes a violation or imminent threat of violation of security policies, security procedures, or acceptable use policies. Information security event.

Incremental backup: A backup that only records any changes made since the last backup.

Indicator: An occurrence or sign that an incident may have occurred or may be in progress.

Industrial control system: An information system used to control industrial processes such as manufacturing, product handling, production, and distribution or to control infrastructure assets.

Information and communications technology: Any information technology, equipment, or interconnected system or subsystem of equipment that processes, transmits, receives, or interchanges data or information.

Information assurance compliance: Overseeing, evaluating, and supporting the documentation, validation, and accreditation processes necessary to assure that new IT systems meet the organization's information assurance and security requirements; ensuring appropriate treatment of risk, compliance, and assurance from internal and external perspectives.

Information assurance: The measures that protect and defend information and information systems by ensuring their availability, integrity, and confidentiality.

Information security event: An event that affects the confidentiality, availability, or integrity of information.

Information security policy: An aggregate of directives, regulations, rules, and practices that prescribe how an organization manages, protects, and distributes information.

Information security: The protection of information and information systems from unauthorized access, use, disclosure, disruption, modification, or destruction in order to provide confidentiality, integrity, and availability.

Information sharing: An exchange of data, information, and/or knowledge to manage risks or respond to incidents.

Information system resilience: The ability of an information system to: continue to operate under adverse conditions or stress, even if in a degraded or debilitated state, while maintaining essential operational capabilities; and recover effectively in a timely manner.

Information system: An integrated set of components for collecting, storing, and processing data and for providing information, knowledge, and digital products, including the network and connected devices.

Information systems security operations: Overseeing the information assurance program of an information system in or outside the network environment.

Information technology: The use of computers, storage, networking and other physical devices, infrastructure and processes to create, process, store, secure and exchange all forms of electronic data.

Information: Organized or classified data.

Insider threat: Current or former employees, contractors, or other business partners who have or had authorized access to an organization's network, system, or data and intentionally misused that access to negatively affect the confidentiality, integrity, or availability of the organization's information or system.

Insider: Any person with authorized access to the organization's resources, including personnel, facilities, information, equipment, networks, or system.

Installation: Malware stored on a target organization's system.

Integrated risk management: The structured approach that enables an enterprise or organization to share risk information and risk analysis and to synchronize independent yet complementary risk management strategies to unify efforts across the organization.

Integrity: Guarding against improper information modification or destruction, and includes ensuring information non-repudiation and authenticity.

Intent: A state of mind or desire to achieve an objective.

Internet protocol: The method by which data is sent from one computer to another on the internet.

Interoperability: The ability of two or more systems or components to exchange information and to use the information that has been exchanged.

Intrusion detection / prevention system: Software that automates the process of monitoring the events occurring in a system and analyzing them for signs of possible incidents and attempting to stop detected possible incidents.

Intrusion detection system: Intrusion detection / prevention system.

Intrusion prevention system: Intrusion detection / prevention system.

Intrusion: An unauthorized act of bypassing the security mechanisms of a network or information system. Penetration.

Inventory: A listing of items including identification and location information.

Investigate: Investigation of cyber events and/or crimes of IT systems, networks, and digital evidence

Investigation: A systematic and formal inquiry into a qualified threat or incident using digital forensics and perhaps other traditional criminal inquiry techniques to determine the events that transpired and to collect evidence. Appling tactics, techniques, and procedures for a full range of investigative tools and processes to include but not limited to interview and interrogation techniques, surveillance, counter surveillance, and surveillance detection, and appropriately balancing the benefits of prosecution versus intelligence gathering.

IP: Either a) internet protocol or, b) intellectual property such as copyright or trade secrets.

IPS: Intrusion detection / prevention system.

Issuing source: An authority responsible for the generation of data, digital evidence (such as assertions), or physical documents that can be used as identity evidence.

IT asset: Asset.

IT: Information technology.

J

Jailbreaking: The process of removing software restrictions on mobile devices to allow for customization or the installation of unauthorized apps.

JavaScript injection: A type of attack that exploits vulnerabilities in web applications to inject malicious code or scripts that can steal sensitive data or compromise the system.

K

KBA: Knowledge-based authentication.

KBP: Knowledge-based proofing.

KBV: Knowledge-based verification.

Kernel: The core component of an operating system that controls system resources and manages hardware and software interactions, often targeted by attackers to gain privileged access to a system.

Keylogger: A type of software or hardware device that records every keystroke made on a computer or mobile device, often used by attackers to steal sensitive information such as passwords or credit card numbers.

Knowledge-based verification: Identity verification method based on knowledge of private information associated with the claimed identity.

Knowledge management: Managing and administering processes and tools that enable the organization to identify, document, and access intellectual capital and information content.

L

Lateral movement: Once in the system, cyberattackers moving to other systems and accounts, in order to gain more control, including higher permissions, more data, or greater access.

Least privilege: The principle of giving a user only the rights to use the system that are required to perform the user's authorized tasks. This principle limits the damage that might result from the accidental, incorrect, or unauthorized use of a system.

Legal advice and advocacy: Legally sound advice and recommendations to leadership and staff on a variety of relevant topics within the pertinent subject domain; advocating legal and policy changes and making a case on behalf of client through a wide range of written and oral work products, including legal briefs and proceedings.

Likelihood: A weighted factor based on a subjective analysis of the probability that a given threat is capable of exploiting a vulnerability.

Log: A data file that records events that occur in a system as they occur, i.e. a record of what happens.

M

MAC: Message authentication code.

Machine learning and evolution: A field concerned with designing and developing artificial intelligence algorithms for automated knowledge discovery and innovation by information systems.

Macro virus: A type of malicious code that attaches itself to documents and uses the macro programming capabilities of the document's application to execute, replicate, and spread or propagate itself.

Malicious actors: Threat agents.

Malicious applet: A small application program that is automatically downloaded and executed and that performs an unauthorized function on an information system.

Malicious code: Program code intended to perform an unauthorized function or process that will have adverse impact on the confidentiality, integrity, or availability of an information system. Includes software, firmware, and scripts.

Malicious insider: Usually a disgruntled employee who steals or destroys the organization's information.

Malicious logic: Hardware, firmware, or software that is intentionally included or inserted in a system to perform an unauthorized function or process that will have adverse impact on the confidentiality, integrity, or availability of an information system.

Malware macros: A small program that can automate tasks in applications which attackers can use to gain access to and harm a system.

Malware: Malicious software designed to infiltrate or damage a system, or steal or harm use computing resources, without the owner's consent. Malware is intended to perform an unauthorized process that will have adverse impact on the confidentiality, integrity, or availability of an information system. Forms include ransomware, virus, spyware (spying), adware (advertising), worm, and Trojan horse.

Managed detection and response: A cybersecurity service that provides continuous monitoring, threat detection, and incident response capabilities for organizations, often using advanced technologies such as machine learning and behavioral analytics.

Man-in-the-middle attack: A cyberattack where the cyberattacker secretly relays and possibly alters the communications between two parties who believe that they are directly communicating with each other, as the cyberattacker has inserted herself between the two parties.

Managed service providers (MSPs): Outsourced contractors who assume the organization's responsibility to perform a range of processes and functions for the purpose of improved operations and reduced budgetary expenditures through the reduction of directly-employed staff.

MDR: Managed Detection and Response.

Memorized secret: A password.

Message authentication code: A cryptographic checksum on data that uses a symmetric key to detect both accidental and intentional modifications of the data. MACs provide authenticity and integrity protection, but not non-repudiation protection.

Metadata: Data that provides information about other data, such as the author, date, or format of a file, often used to organize, search, or manage large datasets, but also contains sensitive information that can be exploited by attackers.

MFA: Multi-factor authentication.

Mitigation: The application of one or more measures to reduce the likelihood of an unwanted occurrence and/or lessen its consequences. Implementing appropriate risk-reduction controls based on risk management priorities and analysis of alternatives.

Mobile code: Executable code that is normally transferred from its source to another computer system for execution. This transfer is often through the network (e.g., JavaScript embedded in a web page) but may transfer through physical media as well.

Moving target defense: The presentation of a dynamic attack surface, increasing an adversary's work factor necessary to probe, attack, or maintain presence in a cyber target.

MSP: Managed service providers.

Multi-factor authentication: Authentication is validated by using a combination of two or more different factors including: something you know (for example, a password), something you have (for example, a physical token), and/or something you are (for example, a fingerprint).

Multi-factor authenticator: An authenticator that provides more than one distinct authentication factor, such as a cryptographic authentication device with an integrated biometric sensor that is required to activate the device.

N

Near field communication: A technology that enables wireless communication and data exchange between devices in close proximity, often used for mobile payments, access control, and other applications.

Network: An open communications medium, typically the Internet, used to transport messages between the claimant and other parties. Unless otherwise stated, no assumptions are made about the network's security; it is assumed to be open and subject to active (e.g., impersonation, man-in-the-middle, session hijacking) and passive (e.g., eavesdropping) attack at any point between the parties (e.g., claimant, verifier, CSP, RP).

Network resilience: The ability of a network to: provide continuous operation (i.e., highly resistant to disruption and able to operate in a degraded mode if damaged); recover effectively if failure does occur; and scale to meet rapid or unpredictable demands.

Network security zone: A networking environment with a well-defined boundary and a standard of cybersecurity to network threats. Types of zones are distinguished by security requirements for interfaces, traffic control, data protection, host configuration control, and network configuration control.

Network services: Installing, configuring, testing, operating, maintaining, and managing networks and their firewalls, including hardware (e.g., hubs, bridges, switches, multiplexers, routers, cables, proxy servers, and protective distributor systems) and software that permit the sharing and transmission of all spectrum transmissions of information to support the security of information and information systems.

Network sniffer: A tool used to capture and analyze network traffic, often used for troubleshooting, network performance optimization, and security analysis or intrusion detection.

NFC: Near Field Communication.

Nmap: A free and open-source network scanner used to discover hosts and services on a network, identify vulnerabilities and misconfigurations, and perform security assessments and penetration testing.

Non-repudiation: A property achieved through cryptographic methods to protect against an individual or entity falsely denying having performed a particular action related to data. Provides the capability to determine whether a given individual took a particular action such as creating information, sending a message, approving information, and receiving a message.

O

Obfuscation: Cyberattackers trying to cover their tracks by laying false trails, compromising data, and clearing logs to confuse or slow down a forensics investigation.

Object: A passive information system-related entity containing or receiving information.

Offensive security: The practice of using hacking techniques and tools to identify and exploit vulnerabilities in computer systems and networks, often used as a defensive mechanism to improve security posture.

Offline: A network disconnected from the internet or a computer or server disconnected from any network, including the internet.

OTP: One-Time Password

One-time password: A temporary password that is valid for only one login session or transaction, often used for two-factor authentication or as a secondary authentication factor.

Online guessing attack: Brute force attack.

Open source intelligence: The collection and analysis of publicly available information and data from open sources, often used in cybersecurity investigations and threat intelligence.

Operate and maintain: Providing the support, administration, and maintenance necessary to ensure effective and efficient IT system performance and security.

Operating system: The software master control application that runs a computer. It is the first computer program loaded when the computer is turned on, and its main component, the kernel, resides in memory at all times. The operating system sets the standards for all application programs (such as the Web server) that run in the computer. The applications communicate with the operating system for most user interface and file management operations.

Operational exercise: An action-based exercise where personnel rehearse reactions to an incident scenario, drawing on their understanding of plans and procedures, roles, and responsibilities. Also referred to as operations-based exercise.

Operational security: Protecting business plans and processes.

Operations technology: The hardware and software systems used to operate industrial control devices.

Orchestration: The automated coordination and management of systems, applications, and services, often used to optimize and streamline IT operations and security.

OS: Operating System.

OSINT: Open Source Intelligence.

Out-of-band: A separate method of communication not using the system. For example, a mobile phone call or Gmail email using a smartphone not connected to the system is "out-of-band".

Outsider threat: A person or group of persons external to an organization who are not authorized to access its assets and pose a potential risk to the organization and its assets.

Oversight and development: Providing leadership, management, direction, and/or development and advocacy so that all individuals and the organization may effectively conduct cybersecurity work.

P

PAD: Presentation attack detection.

Passive attack: An actual assault perpetrated by an intentional threat source that attempts to learn or make use of information from a system, but does not attempt to alter the system, its resources, its data, or its operations.

Passphrase: Instead of a password, a long phrase such as "FenceSoccerHappyBell". A passphrase is similar to a password in usage, but is generally longer for added security.

Password: A string of characters (letters, numbers and other symbols) that are used to authenticate an identity, to verify access authorization or to derive cryptographic keys. A type of authenticator comprised of a character string intended to be memorized or memorable by the subscriber, permitting the subscriber to demonstrate something they know as part of an authentication process.

Pen testing: Penetration testing.

Penetration testing: A method to gain assurance of the security of a system. A cybersecurity professional attempts to breach some or all of the system's security, using the same tools and techniques that a cyberattacker might use.

Penetration: Intrusion.

Perimeter: The boundary between two network security zones through which traffic is routed.

Persistence: A cyberattacker's ability to maintain unauthorized access to a system even after a system restart or shutdown, often achieved by installing malware or modifying system settings.

Personal data: Personally identifiable information.

Personally identifiable information: Information which can be used to distinguish or trace an individual's identity, such as their name, social security number, biometric records, date and place of birth, mother's maiden name, passwords, credit card numbers, driver's license number, and bank account details, alone, or when combined with other personally identifiable information.

Phishing: An attack that uses text, email, or social media to fool users into clicking a malicious link or attachment. An attempt by a third party to solicit confidential information from an individual, group, or organization by mimicking or spoofing, a specific, usually well-known brand, usually for financial gain. Phishers attempt to trick users into disclosing personal data, such as credit card numbers, online banking credentials, and other sensitive information, which they may then use to commit fraudulent acts.

Personal identification number: A memorized secret typically consisting of only decimal digits.

Personal information: Personally identifiable information.

PII: Personally identifiable information.

PIN: Personal identification number.

PKI: Public key infrastructure.

Plaintext: Unencrypted information.

Policy: Statements, rules or assertions that specify correct or expected behavior.

Port: A virtual communication channel used by network protocols to identify specific services or applications running on a computer or network device, often used in firewall configurations to control access to specific ports.

Practice statement: A formal statement of the practices followed by the parties to an authentication process (e.g., CSP or verifier). It usually describes the parties' policies and practices and can become legally binding.

Precursor: An observable occurrence or sign that an attacker may be preparing to cause an incident.

Predictability: Enabling reliable assumptions by individuals, owners, and operators about PII and its processing by an information system.

Presentation attack: Presentation to the biometric data capture subsystem with the goal of interfering with the operation of the biometric system.

Presentation attack detection: Automated determination of a presentation attack. A subset of presentation attack determination methods, referred to as liveness detection, involves measurement and analysis of anatomical characteristics or involuntary or voluntary reactions, in order to determine if a biometric sample is being captured from a living subject present at the point of capture.

Preparedness: The activities to build, sustain, and improve readiness capabilities to prevent, protect against, respond to, and recover from natural or manmade incidents.

Privacy: Protecting personally identifiable information.

Private key: A cryptographic key that must be kept confidential and is used to enable the operation of an asymmetric (public key) cryptographic algorithm. The secret part of an asymmetric key pair that is uniquely associated with an entity.

Privilege escalation: Attackers often need more privileges on a system to get access to more data and system permissions. Once inside, they use techniques to increase their own access privileges, often to the most powerful "administrator" status.

Processing: Operation or set of operations performed upon PII that can include, but is not limited to, the collection, retention, logging, generation, transformation, use, disclosure, transfer, and disposal of PII.

Protect and defend: Identification, analysis, and mitigation of threats to internal IT systems or networks.

Protective DNS: A tool to block employees from visiting potentially malicious domains on the internet.

Protected session: A session wherein messages between two participants are encrypted and integrity is protected using a set of shared secrets called session keys. A protected session is said to be authenticated if, during the session, one participant proves possession of one or more authenticators in addition to the session keys, and if the other party can verify the identity associated with the authenticator(s). If both participants are authenticated, the protected session is said to be mutually authenticated.

Protocol: A set of rules and standards that govern the communication and exchange of data between computers or network devices, often used to ensure compatibility and interoperability between different systems and applications.

Pseudonymous identifier: A meaningless but unique number that does not allow the RP to infer anything regarding the subscriber but which does permit the RP to associate multiple interactions with the subscriber's claimed identity.

Public key certificate: A digital document issued and digitally signed by the private key of a certificate authority that binds an identifier to a subscriber to a public key. The certificate indicates that the subscriber identified in the certificate has sole control and access to the private key.

Public key cryptography: A branch of cryptography in which a cryptographic system or algorithms use two uniquely linked keys: a public key and a private key (a key pair). Asymmetric cryptography, or public key encryption.

Public key encryption: Public key cryptography.

Public key infrastructure: A framework consisting of standards and services to enable secure, encrypted communication and authentication over potentially insecure networks such as the Internet. A framework and services for generating, producing, distributing, controlling, accounting for, and revoking (destroying) public key certificates.

Public key: A cryptographic key that may be widely published and is used to enable the operation of an asymmetric (public key) cryptographic algorithm. The public part of an asymmetric key pair that is uniquely associated with an entity and that may be made public.

R

RaaS: Ransomware as a Service.

Radio frequency identification: A wireless technology used for the identification of objects or people, based on electromagnetic fields. It consists of an RFID tag and an RFID reader, which communicates with each other via radio waves.

Rainbow table: A precomputed table used for reversing cryptographic hash functions, to find the original plaintext input. It is often used by attackers to crack passwords.

Ransomware as a service: A criminal business model used by criminal ransomware software developers in which they lease ransomware in the same way that legitimate software developers lease software as a service (SaaS) products. In this way, regardless of their technical skills, criminals can purchase malware from developers on the dark web. The developers receive a portion of the ransom paid by the victim.

Ransomware: A form of malware designed to block access to a computer system or data, often by encrypting data or programs on systems to extort ransom payments from a victim in exchange for decrypting the information and restoring the victim's access to their system or data.

RAT: Remote Access Trojan.

RCE: Remote Code Execution.

RDP: Remote Desktop Protocol.

Reauthentication: The process of confirming the subscriber's continued presence and intent to be authenticated during an extended usage session.

Reconnaissance: The observation stage where cyberattackers assess, from the outside, to identify targets and tactics. They research and select target companies and systems, including identification of vulnerabilities.

Recover: Develop and implement plans to restore any capabilities or services that were impaired due to a cyberattack.

Recovery: The activities after an incident or event to restore essential services and operations in the short and medium term and fully restore all capabilities in the longer term.

Redaction: The process of removing or obscuring sensitive information from a document or file, to protect the privacy and security of individuals or organizations. It is commonly used in legal and government documents, but also in various industries to protect sensitive data.

Red team exercise: An exercise, reflecting real-world conditions, that is conducted as a simulated attempt by an adversary to attack or exploit vulnerabilities in an organization's information systems.

Red team: A group authorized and organized to emulate a potential adversary's attack or exploitation capabilities against an organization's cybersecurity posture.

Redundancy: Additional or alternative systems, sub-systems, assets, or processes that maintain a degree of overall functionality in case of loss or failure of another system, sub-system, asset, or process.

Registration: Enrollment.

Relying party: An entity that relies upon a verifier's assertion of a subscriber's identity, typically to process a transaction or grant access to information or a system.

Remote: An information exchange between network-connected devices where the information cannot be reliably protected end-to-end by a single organization's security controls.

Remote access trojan: A type of malware that allows a cyberattacker to take control of a victim's computer or device remotely.

Remote code execution: A type of vulnerability that allows a cyberattacker to execute arbitrary code on a remote system or application. This type of vulnerability can be used to take control of systems, steal data, or carry out other malicious activities.

Remote desktop protocol: A method which provides a user with the means to connect to another computer over a network connection. It is commonly used by the IT department to remotely fix computer issues. However, it also is a method for ransomware attacks.

Replay attack: An attack in which the attacker is able to replay previously captured messages (between a legitimate claimant and a verifier) to masquerade as that claimant to the verifier or vice versa.

Replay resistance: The property of an authentication process to resist replay attacks, typically by use of an authenticator output that is valid only for a specific authentication.

Resilience: The ability to adapt to changing conditions and prepare for, withstand, and rapidly recover from disruption.

Respond: Develop and implement action regarding a cyberattack.

Response plan: Incident response plan.

Response: The activities that address the short-term, direct effects of an incident and may also support short-term recovery. In cybersecurity, response encompasses both automated and manual activities.

RFID: Radio Frequency Identification.

Risk analysis: The systematic examination of the components and characteristics of risk.

Risk assessment: The product or process which collects information and assigns values to risks for the purpose of informing priorities, developing or comparing courses of action, and informing decision making. The appraisal of the risks facing an entity, asset, system, or network, organizational operations, individuals, geographic area, other organizations, or society, and includes determining the extent to which adverse circumstances or events could result in harmful consequences.

Risk management: The activity of identifying what information requires what level of protection, and implementing and monitoring that protection.

Risk mitigation: Mitigation.

Risk-based data management: A structured approach to managing risks to data and information by which an organization selects and applies appropriate security controls in compliance with policy and commensurate with the sensitivity and value of the data.

Risk: A function of threats, vulnerabilities, the likelihoods, and the potential impact that a particular cyberattack would have.

Rootkit: A set of software tools with administrator-level access privileges installed on an information system and designed to hide the presence of the tools, maintain the access privileges, and conceal the activities conducted by the tools.

RP: Relying party.

S

Salt: A non-secret value used in a cryptographic process, usually to ensure that the results of computations for one instance cannot be reused by an attacker.

Scans: Activity that seeks to access vulnerabilities.

Script kiddie: An unskilled hacker who relies on pre-written software tools and scripts to launch attacks on networks and computer systems. These individuals lack the technical expertise to create their own tools or write custom scripts, and instead, use off-the-shelf programs to exploit known vulnerabilities.

Secret key: A cryptographic key that is used for both encryption and decryption, enabling the operation of a symmetric key cryptography scheme. Also, a cryptographic algorithm that uses a single key (i.e., a secret key) for both encryption of plaintext and decryption of ciphertext.

Secure sockets layer: TLS/SSL.

Securely provision: Conceptualizing, designing, and building secure IT systems, with responsibility for some aspect of the systems' development.

Security automation: The use of information technology in place of manual processes for cyber incident response and management.

Security incident: Incident.

Security Information and Event Management: A software solution that collects, aggregates, and analyzes security data from various sources in order to detect and respond to security threats.

Security operations center: A centralized unit responsible for monitoring, detecting, analyzing, and responding to security incidents in an organization's IT infrastructure. The SOC typically comprises a team of security analysts and engineers who use various tools and techniques to protect the organization's assets and data from cyber threats.

Security patch: Addresses cybersecurity vulnerabilities to protect the system.

Security policy: A rule or set of rules that govern the acceptable use of an organization's information and services to a level of acceptable risk and the means for protecting the organization's information assets. A rule or set of rules applied to an information system to provide security services.

Security program management: Managing information security (e.g., information security) implications within the organization, specific program, or other area of responsibility, to include strategic, personnel, infrastructure, policy enforcement, emergency planning, security awareness, and other resources (e.g., the role of a Chief Information Security Officer).

Session: A persistent interaction between a subscriber and an endpoint, either an RP or a CSP. A session begins with an authentication event and ends with a session termination event. A session is bound by use of a session secret that the subscriber's software (a browser, application, or OS) can present to the RP to prove association of the session with the authentication event.

Session hijack attack: An attack in which the attacker is able to insert themselves between a claimant and a verifier subsequent to a successful authentication exchange between the latter two parties. The attacker is able to pose as a subscriber to the verifier or vice versa to control session data exchange. Sessions between the claimant and the RP can be similarly compromised.

Shared secret: A secret used in authentication that is known to the subscriber and the verifier.

Side-channel attack: An attack enabled by leakage of information from a physical cryptosystem. Characteristics that could be exploited in a side-channel attack include timing, power consumption, and electromagnetic and acoustic emissions.

SIEM: Security Information and Event Management.

Signature: A recognizable, distinguishing pattern. Types of signatures: attack signature, digital signature, electronic signature.

Single-factor: A characteristic of an authentication system or an authenticator that requires only one authentication factor (i.e., one of: something you know, something you have, or something you are) for successful authentication.

Single sign-on: An authentication method that allows a user to log in with a single identity to access any of several related, but independent, software systems. True single sign-on allows the user to log in once and access services without re-entering any authentication factors.

Situational awareness: Comprehending information about the current and developing security posture and risks, based on information gathered, observation and analysis, and knowledge or experience. Comprehending the current status and security posture with respect to availability, confidentiality, and integrity of networks, systems, users, and data, as well as projecting future states of these.

Sniffing: A technique used by cyberattackers to intercept and monitor network traffic, potentially allowing them to capture sensitive information such as usernames and passwords.

SOC: Security Operations Center.

Social engineering: An attempt to obtain physical or electronic access to business information by manipulating, fooling or conning people. It often takes the form of a fake phone call from "John in the IT Department" asking for a password to enable him "fix" your computer.

Software assurance and security engineering: Developing and coding new or modified computer applications, software, or specialized utility programs following software assurance best practices.

Software assurance: The level of confidence that software is free from vulnerabilities, either intentionally designed into the software or accidentally inserted at any time during its lifecycle, and that the software functions in the intended manner.

Spam: Electronic junk mail to indiscriminately send unsolicited bulk messages.

Spear phishing: A targeted form of phishing that is customized for a specific individual or organization. This is accomplished by researching the target's interests, job role, and relationships to create a convincing message.

Spillage: Data spill, data breach.

Spoof: Using the IP address of another computer or identity of a user to masquerade as a trusted source to gain access to a system. Impersonating, masquerading, piggybacking, and mimicking are forms of spoofing.

Spyware: A form of malware which spies on a user. The aim is to gather information about a person or organization without their knowledge. It may send such information to others without the user's consent and can take over control of a device without the user's knowledge.

SQL: Structured query language.

SSO: Single sign-on.

SSL: TLS/SSL.

State actor: A government which is primarily driven to destroy or disrupt an organization's system or to steal intellectual property and trade secrets for cyberespionage and economic reasons.

Steganography: The practice of hiding secret messages or data within another file or message to avoid detection. This technique involves embedding the data within an image, video, or audio file without changing the file's appearance or functionality.

Strategic planning and policy development: Applying knowledge of priorities to define an entity.

Structured query language injection attack: A type of cyberattack in which a cyberattacker uses a piece of structured query language code to manipulate a database to obtain access to information.

Subject: A person, organization, device, hardware, network, software, or service.

Subscriber: An individual enrolled in the CSP identity service.

Subscriber account: An account established by the CSP containing information and authenticators registered for each subscriber enrolled in the CSP identity service.

Supervised remote identity proofing: A remote identity proofing process that employs physical, technical and procedural measures that provide sufficient confidence that the remote session can be considered equivalent to a physical, in-person identity proofing process.

Supervisory control and data acquisition: A generic name for a computerized system that is capable of gathering and processing data and applying operational controls to geographically dispersed assets over long distances.

Supply chain attacks: A cyberattacker infiltrates a service supply organization and infects their system with ransomware, often through a seemingly normal software update.

Supply chain risk management: The process of identifying, analyzing, and assessing supply chain risk and accepting, avoiding, transferring or controlling it to an acceptable level considering associated costs and benefits of any actions taken.

Supply chain: A system of organizations, people, activities, information and resources, for creating and moving products including product components and/or services from suppliers through to their customers.

Symmetric cryptography: A branch of cryptography in which a cryptographic system or algorithms use the same secret key (a shared secret key).

Symmetric encryption algorithm: Symmetric cryptography.

Symmetric key: A cryptographic key that is used to perform both the cryptographic operation and its inverse, for example to encrypt plaintext and decrypt ciphertext, or create a message authentication code and to verify the code. Also, a cryptographic algorithm that uses a single key (i.e., a secret key) for both encryption of plaintext and decryption of ciphertext.

Synthetic identity fraud: The use of a combination of personally identifiable information (PII) to fabricate a person or entity in order to commit a dishonest act for personal or financial gain.

System administration: Installing, configuring, troubleshooting, and maintaining server configurations (hardware and software) to ensure their confidentiality, integrity, and availability; also managing accounts, firewalls, and patches; responsibility for access control, passwords, and account creation and administration.

System integrity: The attribute of an information system when it performs its intended function in an unimpaired manner, free from deliberate or inadvertent unauthorized manipulation of the system.

System: An information system.

Systems development: Working on the development phases of the systems development lifecycle.

Systems requirements planning: Consulting with customers to gather and evaluate functional requirements and translates these requirements into technical solutions; providing guidance to customers about applicability of information systems to meet business needs.

Systems security analysis: Conducting the integration/testing, operations, and maintenance of systems security.

Systems security architecture: Developing system concepts and working on the capabilities phases of the systems development lifecycle; translating technology and environmental conditions (e.g., law and regulation) into system and security designs and processes.

T

Tabletop exercise: A discussion-based exercise where personnel meet in a classroom setting or breakout groups and are presented with a scenario to validate the content of plans, procedures, policies, cooperative agreements or other information for managing an incident.

Tailored trustworthy space: A cyberspace environment that provides a user with confidence in its security, using automated mechanisms to ascertain security conditions and adjust the level of security based on the user's context and in the face of an evolving range of threats.

Targets: Applying current knowledge of one or more regions, countries, non-state entities, and/or technologies.

Technology research and development: Conducting technology assessment and integration processes; providing and supporting a prototype capability and/or evaluating its utility.

Test and evaluation: Developing and conducting tests of systems to evaluate compliance with specifications and requirements by applying principles and methods for cost-effective planning, evaluating, verifying, and validating of technical, functional, and performance characteristics (including interoperability) of systems or elements of systems incorporating information technology.

Threat actor: Threat agent.

Threat agent: An individual, group, organization, or government that conducts or has the intent to conduct detrimental activities.

Threat analysis: The detailed evaluation of the characteristics of individual threats. Identifying and assessing the capabilities and activities of criminals or foreign intelligence entities; producing findings to help initialize or support law enforcement and counterintelligence investigations or activities.

Threat assessment: The product or process of identifying or evaluating entities, actions, or occurrences, whether natural or man-made, that have or indicate the potential to harm life, information, operations, and/or property.

Threat: A circumstance or event with the potential to adversely impact organizational operations (including mission, functions, or reputation), organizational assets, individuals, other organizations, through a system via unauthorized access, destruction, disclosure, modification of information, and/or denial of service.

Threat intelligence: Information about potential or current cyber threats and vulnerabilities, often collected and analyzed by security researchers, vendors, or government agencies to improve cybersecurity defenses and response.

Ticket: In access control, data that authenticates the identity of a client or a service and, together with a temporary encryption key (a session key), forms a credential.

TLS/SSL: Transport Layer Security/Secure Sockets Layer encryption.

Token: Authenticator.

Traceroute: A command-line tool used to trace the path that network packets take between a source and destination device, often used to troubleshoot network connectivity issues.

Traffic light protocol: A set of designations employing four colors (red, amber, green, and white) used to ensure that sensitive information is shared with the correct audience.

Transaction: A discrete event between a user and a system that supports a business or programmatic purpose. A digital system may have multiple categories or types of transactions, which may require separate analysis within the overall digital identity risk assessment.

Transport layer security/secure sockets layer encryption: A method to encrypt communications between a computer and server, primarily between web browsers and websites.

Trojan horse: A computer program that appears to have a useful function, but also has a hidden and potentially malicious function that evades security mechanisms, sometimes by exploiting legitimate authorizations of a system entity that invokes the program.

Trust anchor: A public or symmetric key that is trusted because it is directly built into hardware or software, or securely provisioned via out-of-band means, rather than because it is vouched for by another trusted entity (e.g. in a public key certificate). A trust anchor may have name or policy constraints limiting its scope.

Two factor authentication: A form of multi-factor authentication.

U

Unauthorized access: Gaining illicit remote or physical access to a system.

Universal serial bus: Type of standard cable, connector, and protocol for connecting computers, electronic devices, and power sources.

Uptime: The amount of time that a system or service is available and operational. It is a measure of the reliability and stability of a system.

URL: Uniform resource locator, i.e. "http://website.com/doc.html".

URL spoofing: A technique used by cyberattackers to disguise a malicious website as a legitimate one. It involves using a similar-looking domain name or URL to trick users into visiting the fake site.

Usability: The extent to which a product can be used by specified users to achieve specified goals with effectiveness, efficiency, and satisfaction in a specified context of use.

USB: Universal Serial Bus.

USB rubber ducky: A type of programmable USB device that can simulate keyboard input to automate tasks or execute commands on a computer system.

User: The person who is interacting with a computer or other device.

V

Validation: The process or act of checking and confirming that the evidence and attributes supplied by an applicant are authentic, accurate and associated with a real-life identity. Specifically, evidence validation is the process or act of checking that presented evidence is authentic, current, and issued from an acceptable source; attribute validation is the process or act of confirming that a set of attributes are accurate and associated with a real-life identity.

Vector: Attack method.

Vector: Method of cyberattack.

Verification: The process or act of confirming that the applicant holds the claimed identity represented by the validated identity attributes and associated evidence.

Verifier: An entity that verifies the claimant's identity by verifying the claimant's possession and control of one or more authenticators using an authentication protocol. To do this, the verifier needs to confirm the binding of the authenticators with the subscriber account and check that the subscriber account is active.

Verifier impersonation: Phishing.

Virtual private network: An application which extends a private network across a public network and enables users to send and receive data across shared or public networks as securely as if their computing devices were directly connected to the private network.

Virus: A computer program that can replicate itself, infect a computer without permission or knowledge of the user, and then spread or propagate to another computer.

VPN: Virtual private network.

Vulnerability assessment and management: Conducting assessments of threats and vulnerabilities, determining deviations from acceptable configurations, organization or local policy, assessing the level of risk, and develops and/or recommending appropriate mitigation countermeasures in operational and non-operational situations.

Vulnerability: A weakness in a system, system security procedures, internal controls, or implementation that could be exploited by a cyberattacker to harm an organization.

W

Watering hole attack: A type of cyberattack that targets a specific group of users by infecting websites that they are likely to visit. The attacker compromises a website and installs malware, which is then downloaded by the visitors of the website.

Weakness: A shortcoming or imperfection in software code, design, architecture, or deployment that, under proper conditions, could become a vulnerability or contribute to the introduction of vulnerabilities.

Weaponization: Use of remote access malware and exploits to create a deliverable ransomware payload.

Web scraping: The process of automatically extracting data from websites. It is often used for data mining or research purposes, but can also be used for malicious purposes such as stealing data or intellectual property.

Web-based attack: A type of cyberattack that targets vulnerabilities in web applications. This can include injecting malicious code into web pages, exploiting vulnerabilities in the underlying web server, or stealing sensitive information from web applications.

White hat: In contrast to black bat, programmers who seek to access systems to test the system's capabilities, and report vulnerabilities to the organization or authorities for fixing. They often refer to themselves as cybersecurity researchers and seek to be paid fairly for their services. They are not criminals.

White team: A group responsible for refereeing an engagement between a Red Team of mock attackers and a Blue Team of actual defenders of information systems.

Wi-Fi pineapple: A wireless networking device used for penetration testing and hacking. It is designed to mimic a legitimate wireless access point and capture sensitive information from unsuspecting users.

Wipe: Electronically erase by completely writing over the entire storage device a sufficient number of times.

Work factor: An estimate of the effort or time needed by a potential adversary, with specified expertise and resources, to overcome a protective measure.

Worm: A self-replicating, self-propagating, self-contained program that uses networking mechanisms to spread itself.

X

XSS: Cross-site scripting.

Z

Zero-day: A software vulnerability that is unknown to the software vendor and has not yet been patched. Cyberattackers can exploit zero-day vulnerabilities to launch targeted attacks that can compromise user data and systems.

Zeroize: Overwrite a memory location with data consisting entirely of bits with the value zero (or other random values) so that the data is destroyed and not recoverable. This is often contrasted with deletion methods that merely destroy reference to data within a file system rather than destroying the data itself.

Zero-knowledge password protocol: A password-based authentication protocol that allows a claimant to authenticate to a verifier without revealing the password to the verifier.

Zero trust: A security model that requires strict identity verification for all users, devices, and applications attempting to access a network. It assumes that every device, user, and application is a potential threat and employs multiple layers of security to protect against data breaches and cyberattacks.

Cybersecurity for Small Business

U.S. Federal Trade Commission

CYBERSECURITY BASICS

Cyber criminals target companies of all sizes.

Knowing some cybersecurity basics and putting them in practice will help you protect your business and reduce the risk of a cyber attack.

PROTECT —
YOUR FILES & DEVICES

Update your software

This includes your apps, web browsers, and operating systems. Set updates to happen automatically.

Secure your files

Back up important files offline, on an external hard drive, or in the cloud. Make sure you store your paper files securely, too.

Require passwords

Use passwords for all laptops, tablets, and smartphones. Don't leave these devices unattended in public places.

Encrypt devices

Encrypt devices and other media that contain sensitive personal information. This includes laptops, tablets, smartphones, removable drives, backup tapes, and cloud storage solutions.

Use multi-factor authentication

Require multi-factor authentication to access areas of your network with sensitive information. This requires additional steps beyond logging in with a password — like a temporary code on a smartphone or a key that's inserted into a computer.

PROTECT YOUR WIRELESS NETWORK ——

Secure your router

Change the default name and password, turn off remote management, and log out as the administrator once the router is set up.

Use at least WPA2 encryption

Make sure your router offers WPA2 or WPA3 encryption, and that it's turned on. Encryption protects information sent over your network so it can't be read by outsiders.

MAKE ——
SMART SECURITY
YOUR BUSINESS AS USUAL

Require strong passwords

A strong password is at least 12 characters that are a mix of numbers, symbols, and capital lowercase letters.

Never reuse passwords and don't share them on the phone, in texts, or by email.

Limit the number of unsuccessful log-in attempts to limit password-guessing attacks.

Train all staff

Create a culture of security by implementing a regular schedule of employee training. Update employees as you find out about new risks and vulnerabilities. If employees don't attend, consider blocking their access to the network.

Have a plan

Have a plan for saving data, running the business, and notifying customers if you experience a breach. The FTC's *Data Breach Response: A Guide for Business* gives steps you can take. You can find it at FTC.gov/DataBreach.

CYBERSECURITY FOR
SMALL BUSINESS

Understanding
THE NIST CYBERSECURITY FRAMEWORK

You may have heard about the NIST Cybersecurity Framework, but what exactly is it?

And does it apply to you?

NIST is the National Institute of Standards and Technology at the U.S. Department of Commerce. The NIST Cybersecurity Framework helps businesses of all sizes better understand, manage, and reduce their cybersecurity risk and protect their networks and data. The Framework is voluntary. It gives your business an outline of best practices to help you decide where to focus your time and money for cybersecurity protection.

You can put the NIST Cybersecurity Framework to work in your business in these five areas: Identify, Protect, Detect, Respond, and Recover.

1. IDENTIFY ——

Make a list of all equipment, software, and data you use, including laptops, smartphones, tablets, and point-of-sale devices.

Create and share a company cybersecurity policy that covers:

 Roles and responsibilities for employees, vendors, and anyone else with access to sensitive data.

 Steps to take to protect against an attack and limit the damage if one occurs.

2. PROTECT ——

- Control who logs on to your network and uses your computers and other devices.

- Use security software to protect data.

- Encrypt sensitive data, at rest and in transit.

- Conduct regular backups of data.

- Update security software regularly, automating those updates if possible.

- Have formal policies for safely disposing of electronic files and old devices.

- Train everyone who uses your computers, devices, and network about cybersecurity. You can help employees understand their personal risk in addition to their crucial role in the workplace.

CYBERSECURITY FOR
SMALL BUSINESS

3. DETECT ——

Monitor your computers for unauthorized personnel access, devices (like USB drives), and software.

Check your network for unauthorized users or connections.

Investigate any unusual activities on your network or by your staff.

4. RESPOND ——

Have a plan for:

- Notifying customers, employees, and others whose data may be at risk.
- Keeping business operations up and running.
- Reporting the attack to law enforcement and other authorities.

- Investigating and containing an attack.
- Updating your cybersecurity policy and plan with lessons learned.
- Preparing for inadvertent events (like weather emergencies) that may put data at risk.

Test your plan regularly.

5. RECOVER —

After an attack:

Repair and restore the equipment and parts of your network that were affected.

Keep employees and customers informed of your response and recovery activities.

For more information on the NIST Cybersecurity Framework and resources for small businesses, go to NIST.gov/CyberFramework and NIST.gov/Programs-Projects/Small-Business-Corner-SBC.

CYBERSECURITY FOR
SMALL BUSINESS

PHYSICAL SECURITY

Cybersecurity begins with strong physical security.

Lapses in physical security can expose sensitive company data to identity theft, with potentially serious consequences. For example:

An employee accidentally leaves a flash drive on a coffeehouse table. When he returns hours later to get it, the drive — with hundreds of Social Security numbers saved on it — is gone.

Another employee throws stacks of old company bank records into a trash can, where a criminal finds them after business hours.

A burglar steals files and computers from your office after entering through an unlocked window.

HOW TO **PROTECT** EQUIPMENT & PAPER FILES

Here are some tips for protecting information in paper files and on hard drives, flash drives, laptops, point-of-sale devices, and other equipment.

Store securely

When paper files or electronic devices contain sensitive information, store them in a locked cabinet or room.

Limit physical access

When records or devices contain sensitive data, allow access only to those who need it.

Send reminders

Remind employees to put paper files in locked file cabinets, log out of your network and applications, and never leave files or devices with sensitive data unattended.

Keep stock

Keep track of and secure any devices that collect sensitive customer information. Only keep files and data you need and know who has access to them.

HOW TO **PROTECT** DATA ON YOUR DEVICES ———

A burglary, lost laptop, stolen mobile phone, or misplaced flash drive — all can happen due to lapses in physical security. But they're less likely to result in a data breach if information on those devices is protected. Here are a few ways to do that:

Require complex passwords

Require passwords that are long, complex, and unique. And make sure that these passwords are stored securely. Consider using a password manager.

Use multi-factor authentication

Require multi-factor authentication to access areas of your network with sensitive information. This requires additional steps beyond logging in with a password — like a temporary code on a smartphone or a key that's inserted into a computer.

Limit login attempts

Limit the number of incorrect login attempts allowed to unlock devices. This will help protect against intruders.

Encrypt

Encrypt portable media, including laptops and thumb drives, that contain sensitive information. Encrypt any sensitive data you send outside of the company, like to an accountant or a shipping service.

Include physical security in your regular employee trainings and communications. Remind employees to:

Shred documents

Always shred documents with sensitive information before throwing them away.

Erase data correctly

Use software to erase data before donating or discarding old computers, mobile devices, digital copiers, and drives. Don't rely on "delete" alone. That does not actually remove the file from the computer.

Promote security practices in all locations

Maintain security practices even if working remotely from home or on business travel.

Know the response plan

All staff should know what to do if equipment or paper files are lost or stolen, including whom to notify and what to do next. Use *Data Breach Response: A Guide for Business* for help creating a response plan. You can find it at FTC.gov/DataBreach.

CYBERSECURITY FOR
SMALL BUSINESS

HOW TO **PROTECT** YOUR BUSINESS

Have a plan
How would your business stay up and running after a ransomware attack?
Put this plan in writing and share it with everyone who needs to know.

Back up your data
Regularly save important files to a drive or server that's not connected to your network.
Make data backup part of your routine business operations.

Keep your security up to date
Always install the latest patches and updates. Look for additional means of protection,
like email authentication, and intrusion prevention software, and set them to update
automatically on your computer. On mobile devices, you may have to do it manually.

Alert your staff
Teach them how to avoid phishing scams and show them some of the common ways
computers and devices become infected. Include tips for spotting and protecting against
ransomware in your regular orientation and training.

WHAT TO DO IF YOU'RE
ATTACKED

Limit the damage
Immediately disconnect the infected computers or devices from your network. If your data has been stolen, take steps to protect your company and notify those who might be affected.

Contact the authorities
Report the attack right away to your local FBI office.

Notify customers
If your data or personal information was compromised, make sure you notify the affected parties – they could be at risk of identity theft. Find information on how to do that at *Data Breach Response: A Guide for Business*. You can find it at FTC.gov/DataBreach.

Keep your business running
Now's the time to implement that plan. Having data backed up will help.

Should I pay the ransom?
Law enforcement doesn't recommend that, but it's up to you to determine whether the risks and costs of paying are worth the possibility of getting your files back. However, paying the ransom may not guarantee you get your data back.

CYBERSECURITY FOR
SMALL BUSINESS

RANSOMWARE

Someone in your company gets an email.

It looks legitimate — but with one click on a link, or one download of an attachment, everyone is locked out of your network. That link downloaded software that holds your data hostage. That's a ransomware attack.

The attackers ask for money or cryptocurrency, but even if you pay, you don't know if the cybercriminals will keep your data or destroy your files. Meanwhile, the information you need to run your business and sensitive details about your customers, employees, and company are now in criminal hands. Ransomware can take a serious toll on your business.

HOW IT
HAPPENS

Criminals can start a ransomware attack in a variety of ways.

Scam emails
with links and attachments that put your data and network at risk. These phishing emails make up most ransomware attacks.

Server vulnerabilities
which can be exploited by hackers.

Infected websites
that automatically download malicious software onto your computer.

Online ads
that contain malicious code — even on websites you know and trust.

You get an email that looks like it's from someone you know.

It seems to be from one of your company's vendors and asks that you click on a link to update your business account. Should you click? Maybe it looks like it's from your boss and asks for your network password. Should you reply? In either case, probably not. These may be phishing attempts.

HOW

PHISHING WORKS

You get an email or text

It seems to be from someone you know, and it asks you to click a link, or give your password, business bank account, or other sensitive information.

It looks real

It's easy to spoof logos and make up fake email addresses. Scammers use familiar company names or pretend to be someone you know.

It's urgent

The message pressures you to act now — or something bad will happen.

What happens next

If you click on a link, scammers can install ransomware or other programs that can lock you out of your data and spread to the entire company network. If you share passwords, scammers now have access to all those accounts.

WHAT YOU CAN DO

Before you click on a link or share any of your sensitive business information:

Check it out

Look up the website or phone number for the company or person behind the text or email. Make sure that you're getting the real company and not about to download malware or talk to a scammer.

Talk to someone

Talking to a colleague might help you figure out if the request is real or a phishing attempt.

Make a call if you're not sure

Pick up the phone and call that vendor, colleague, or client who sent the email. Confirm that they really need information from you. Use a number you know to be correct, not the number in the email or text.

CYBERSECURITY FOR
SMALL BUSINESS

HOW TO ———
PROTECT
YOUR BUSINESS

Back up your data

Regularly back up your data and make sure those backups are not connected to the network. That way, if a phishing attack happens and hackers get to your network, you can restore your data. Make data backup part of your routine business operations.

Keep your security up to date

Always install the latest patches and updates. Look for additional means of protection, like email authentication and intrusion prevention software, and set them to update automatically on your computers. On mobile devices, you may have to do it manually.

Alert your staff

Share with them this information. Keep in mind that phishing scammers change their tactics often, so make sure you include tips for spotting the latest phishing schemes in your regular training.

Deploy a safety net

Use email authentication technology to help prevent phishing emails from reaching your company's inboxes in the first place.

WHAT IF YOU FALL FOR A
PHISHING SCHEME

Alert others

Talk to your colleagues and share your experience. Phishing attacks often happen to more than one person in a company.

Limit the damage

Immediately change any compromised passwords and disconnect from the network any computer or device that's infected with malware.

Follow your company's procedures

These may include notifying specific people in your organization or contractors that help you with IT.

Notify customers

If your data or personal information was compromised, make sure you notify the affected parties — they could be at risk of identity theft. Find information on how to do that at *Data Breach Response: A Guide for Business* (FTC.gov/DataBreach).

Report it

Forward phishing emails to spam@uce. gov (an address used by the FTC) and to reportphishing@apwg.org (an address used by the Anti-Phishing Working Group, which includes ISPs, security vendors, financial institutions, and law enforcement agencies). Let the company or person that was impersonated know about the phishing scheme. And report it to the FTC at FTC.gov/Complaint.

CYBERSECURITY FOR
SMALL BUSINESS

BUSINESS EMAIL IMPOSTERS

A scammer sets up an email address that looks like it's from your company.

Then the scammer sends out messages using that email address. This practice is called spoofing, and the scammer is what we call a business email imposter.

Scammers do this to get passwords and bank account numbers or to get someone to send them money. When this happens, your company has a lot to lose. Customers and partners might lose trust and take their business elsewhere — and your business could then lose money.

HOW TO **PROTECT** YOUR BUSINESS ———

Use email authentication

When you set up your business's email, make sure the email provider offers email authentication technology. That way, when you send an email from your company's server, the receiving servers can confirm that the email is really from you. If it's not, the receiving servers may block the email and foil a business email imposter.

Keep your security up to date

Always install the latest patches and updates. Set them to update automatically on your network. Look for additional means of protection, like intrusion prevention software, which checks your network for suspicious activity and sends you alerts if it finds any.

Train your staff

Teach them how to avoid phishing scams and show them some of the common ways attackers can infect computers and devices with malware. Include tips for spotting and protecting against cyber threats in your regular employee trainings and communications.

WHAT TO DO ────
IF SOMEONE SPOOFS YOUR COMPANY'S EMAIL

Report it

Report the scam to local law enforcement, the FBI's Internet Crime Complaint Center at IC3.gov, and the FTC at FTC.gov/Complaint. You can also forward phishing emails to spam@uce.gov (an address used by the FTC) and to reportphishing@apwg.org (an address used by the Anti-Phishing Working Group, which includes ISPs, security vendors, financial institutions, and law enforcement agencies).

Notify your customers

If you find out scammers are impersonating your business, tell your customers as soon as possible — by mail, email, or social media. If you email your customers, send an email without hyperlinks. You don't want your notification email to look like a phishing scam. Remind customers not to share any personal information through email or text. If your customers' data was stolen, direct them to IdentityTheft.gov to get a recovery plan.

Alert your staff

Use this experience to update your security practices and train your staff about cyber threats.

CYBERSECURITY FOR
SMALL BUSINESS

TECH SUPPORT SCAMS

You get a phone call, pop-up, or email telling you there's a problem with your computer.

Often, scammers are behind these calls, pop-up messages, and emails. They want to get your money, personal information, or access to your files. This can harm your network, put your data at risk, and damage your business.

HOW THE SCAM WORKS

The scammers may pretend to be from a well-known tech company, such as Microsoft. They use lots of technical terms to convince you that the problems with your computer are real. They may ask you to open some files or run a scan on your computer — and then tell you those files or the scan results show a problem...but there isn't one.

The scammers may then:

 Ask you to give them remote access to your computer — which lets them access all information stored on it, and on any network connected to it

 Install malware that gives them access to your computer and sensitive data, like user names and passwords

 Try to sell you software or repair services that are worthless or available elsewhere for free

 Try to enroll you in a worthless computer maintenance or warranty program

 Ask for credit card information so they can bill you for phony services or services available elsewhere for free

 Direct you to websites and ask you to enter credit card, bank account, and other personal information

CYBERSECURITY FOR
SMALL BUSINESS

HOW TO **PROTECT** YOUR BUSINESS ──────

If a caller says your computer has a problem, hang up. A tech support call you don't expect is a scam — even if the number is local or looks legitimate. These scammers use fake caller ID information to look like local businesses or trusted companies.

If you get a pop-up message to call tech support, ignore it. Some pop-up messages about computer issues are legitimate, but do not call a number or click on a link that appears in a pop-up message warning you of a computer problem.

If you're worried about a virus or other threat, call your security software company directly, using the phone number on its website, the sales receipt, or the product packaging. Or consult a trusted security professional.

Never give someone your password, and don't give remote access to your computer to someone who contacts you unexpectedly.

WHAT TO DO IF YOU'RE
SCAMMED ──────

If you shared your password with a scammer, change it on every account that uses this password. Remember to use unique passwords for each account and service. Consider using a password manager.

Get rid of malware. Update or download legitimate security software. Scan your computer, and delete anything the software says is a problem. If you need help, consult a trusted security professional.

If the affected computer is connected to your network, you or a security professional should check the entire network for intrusions.

If you bought bogus services, ask your credit card company to reverse the charges, and check your statement for any charges you didn't approve. Keep checking your credit card statements to make sure the scammer doesn't try to re-charge you every month.

Report the attack right away to the FTC at FTC.gov/Complaint.

CYBERSECURITY FOR
SMALL BUSINESS

CYBER INSURANCE

Recovering from a cyber attack can be costly.

Cyber insurance is one option that can help protect your business against losses resulting from a cyber attack. If you're thinking about cyber insurance, discuss with your insurance agent what policy would best fit your company's needs, including whether you should go with first-party coverage, third-party coverage, or both. Here are some general tips to consider.

WHAT SHOULD YOUR
CYBER INSURANCE POLICY
COVER?

Make sure your policy includes coverage for:

☐ Data breaches (like incidents involving theft of personal information)

☐ Cyber attacks on your data held by vendors and other third parties

☐ Terrorist acts

☐ Cyber attacks (like breaches of your network)

☐ Cyber attacks that occur anywhere in the world (not only in the United States)

Also, consider whether your cyber insurance provider will:

☐ Defend you in a lawsuit or regulatory investigation (look for "duty to defend" wording)

☐ Provide coverage in excess of any other applicable insurance you have

☐ Offer a breach hotline that's available every day of the year at all times

SMALL BUSINESS

WHAT IS ————

FIRST-PARTY COVERAGE
AND WHAT SHOULD YOU LOOK FOR?

First-party cyber coverage protects your data, including employee and customer information. This coverage typically includes your business's costs related to:

- ☐ Legal counsel to determine your notification and regulatory obligations
- ☐ Customer notification and call center services
- ☐ Crisis management and public relations
- ☐ Forensic services to investigate the breach

- ☐ Recovery and replacement of lost or stolen data
- ☐ Lost income due to business interruption
- ☐ Cyber extortion and fraud
- ☐ Fees, fines, and penalties related to the cyber incident

WHAT IS ————

THIRD-PARTY COVERAGE
AND WHAT SHOULD YOU LOOK FOR?

Third-party cyber coverage generally protects you from liability if a third party brings claims against you. This coverage typically includes:

- ☐ Payments to consumers affected by the breach
- ☐ Claims and settlement expenses relating to disputes or lawsuits
- ☐ Losses related to defamation and copyright or trademark infringement

- ☐ Costs for litigation and responding to regulatory inquiries
- ☐ Other settlements, damages, and judgments
- ☐ Accounting costs

More insurance resources for small businesses available at www.insureuonline.org/smallbusiness

CYBERSECURITY FOR
SMALL BUSINESS

EMAIL AUTHENTICATION

Email authentication technology makes it a lot harder for a scammer to send phishing emails that look like they're from your company.

Using email authentication technology makes it a lot harder for scammers to send phishing emails. This technology allows a receiving server to verify an email from your company and block emails from an imposter — or send them to a quarantine folder and then notify you about them.

WHAT TO KNOW

Some web host providers let you set up your company's business email using your domain name (which you may think of as your website name). Your domain name might look like this: yourbusiness.com. And your email may look like this: name@yourbusiness.com. Without email authentication, scammers can use that domain name to send emails that look like they're from your business. If your business email uses your company's domain name, make sure that your email provider has these three email authentication tools:

Sender Policy Framework (SPF)

tells other servers which servers are allowed to send emails using your business's domain name. So when you send an email from name@yourbusiness. com, the receiving server can confirm that the sending server is on an approved list. If it is, the receiving server lets the email through. If it can't find a match, the email can be flagged as suspicious.

Domain Keys Identified Mail (DKIM)

puts a digital signature on outgoing mail so servers can verify that an email from your domain actually was sent from your organization's servers and hasn't been tampered with in transit.

Domain-based Message Authentication, Reporting & Conformance (DMARC)

is the essential third tool for email authentication. SPF and DKIM verify the address the server uses "behind the scenes." DMARC verifies that this address matches the "from" address you see. It also lets you tell other servers what to do when they get an email that looks like it came from your domain, but the receiving server has reason to be suspicious (based on SPF or DKIM). You can have other servers reject the email, flag it as spam, or take no action. You also can set up DMARC so that you're notified when this happens.

It takes some expertise to configure these tools so that they work as intended and don't block legitimate email. Make sure that your email hosting provider can set them up if you don't have the technical knowledge. If they can't, or don't include that in their service agreement, consider getting another provider.

CYBERSECURITY FOR
SMALL BUSINESS

WHAT TO DO IF YOUR ——
EMAIL IS SPOOFED

Email authentication helps keep your business's email from being used in phishing schemes because it notifies you if someone spoofs your company's email. If you get that notification, take these actions:

Report it

Report the scam to local law enforcement, the FBI's Internet Crime Complaint Center at IC3.gov, and the FTC at FTC.gov/Complaint. You also can forward phishing emails to spam@uce.gov (an address used by the FTC) and to reportphishing@apwg.org (an address used by the Anti-Phishing Working Group, which includes ISPs, security vendors, financial institutions, and law enforcement agencies).

Notify your customers

If you find out scammers are impersonating your business, tell your customers as soon as possible — by mail, email, or social media. If you email your customers, send an email without hyperlinks: you don't want your notification email to look like a phishing scam. Remind customers not to share any personal information through email or text. And if your customers' data was stolen, direct them to IdentityTheft.gov to get a recovery plan.

Alert your staff

Use this experience to update your security practices and train your staff about cyber threats.

CYBERSECURITY FOR
SMALL BUSINESS

VENDOR SECURITY

Your business vendors may have access to sensitive information.

Make sure those vendors are securing their own computers and networks. For example, what if your accountant, who has all your financial data, loses his laptop? Or a vendor whose network is connected to yours gets hacked? The result: your business data and your customers' personal information may end up in the wrong hands — putting your business and your customers at risk.

HOW TO **MONITOR** YOUR VENDORS

Put it in writing

Include provisions for security in your vendor contracts, like a plan to evaluate and update security controls, since threats change. Make the security provisions that are critical to your company non-negotiable.

Verify compliance

Establish processes so you can confirm that vendors follow your rules. Don't just take their word for it.

Make changes as needed

Cybersecurity threats change rapidly. Make sure your vendors keep their security up to date.

HOW TO **PROTECT** YOUR BUSINESS ——

Control access

Put controls on databases with sensitive information. Limit access to a need-to-know basis, and only for the amount of time a vendor needs to do a job.

Use multi-factor authentication

This makes vendors take additional steps beyond logging in with a password to access your network — like a temporary code on a smartphone or a key that's inserted into a computer.

Secure your network

Require strong passwords: at least 12 characters with a mix of numbers, symbols, and both capital and lowercase letters. Never reuse passwords, don't share them, and limit the number of unsuccessful log-in attempts to limit password-guessing attacks.

Safeguard your data

Use properly configured, strong encryption. This protects sensitive information as it's transferred and stored.

WHAT TO DO IF A VENDOR HAS A ——
DATA BREACH

Contact the authorities

Report the attack right away to your local police department. If they're not familiar with investigating information compromises, contact your local FBI office.

Notify customers

If your data or personal information was compromised, make sure you notify the affected parties — they could be at risk of identity theft. Find information on how to do that at *Data Breach Response: A Guide for Business*. Find it at FTC.gov/DataBreach.

Confirm the vendor has a fix

Make sure that the vendor fixes the vulnerabilities and ensures that your information will be safe going forward, if your business decides to continue using the vendor.

CYBERSECURITY FOR
SMALL BUSINESS

HIRING A WEB HOST

You may want a new or upgraded website for your business.

But if you don't have the skills to set up the web presence you want, you may want to hire a web host provider to do it for you. Whether you're upgrading a website or launching a new business, there are many web-hosting options. When comparing services, security should be a top concern.

WHAT TO LOOK FOR

Transport Layer Security (TLS)

The service you choose should include TLS, which will help to protect your customers' privacy. (You may have heard of its predecessor, Secure Sockets Layer, or SSL.) TLS helps make sure that your customers get to your real website when they type your URL into the address bar. When TLS is correctly implemented on your website, your URL will begin with https://.

TLS also helps make sure the information sent to your website is encrypted. That's especially important if you ask customers for sensitive information, like credit card numbers or passwords.

Email authentication

Some web host providers let you set up your company's business email using your domain name (that's part of your URL, and what you may think of as your website name). Your domain name might look like this: yourbusiness.com. And your email may look like this: name@yourbusiness.com. If you don't have email authentication, scammers can impersonate that domain name and send emails that look like they're from your business.

When your business email is set up using your company's domain name, make sure that your web host can give you these three email authentication tools:

- Sender Policy Framework (SPF)
- Domain Keys Identified Mail (DKIM)
- Domain-based Message Authentication, Reporting & Conformance (DMARC)

WHAT TO ——— LOOK FOR

Software updates

Many web host providers offer pre-built websites or software packages designed to make it quick and easy to set up your company's website. As with any software, it is essential that you use the latest versions with up-to-date security patches. Make sure you know how to keep the website's software up to date, or whether the web host provider will do this for you.

Website management

If a web host provider is managing your website, you may have to go through that provider to make any changes — though you may be able to log in and make some changes yourself. Some web host providers may instead offer you the option of managing the website on your own. It's important to clarify from the beginning who will manage the website after it's built.

WHAT TO ASK ———

When you're hiring a web host provider, ask these questions to make sure you're helping protect your customer information and your business data.

☐ Is TLS included in the hosting plan? paid add-on? Will I set it up myself or will you help me set it up?

☐ Are the most up-to-date software versions available with your service, and will you keep software updated? If it's my responsibility to keep software updated, is it easy for me to do?

☐ Can my business email use my business website name? If so, can you help me set up SPF, DKIM, and DMARC email authentication technology? (If not, consider looking for a provider that does.)

☐ After the website is set up, who will be able to make changes to it? Will I have to go through you? Will I be able to log in and make changes on my own? If I can log in to make changes, is multi-factor authentication available?

SECURE
REMOTE ACCESS

Employees and vendors may need to connect to your network remotely.

Put your network's security first. Make employees and vendors follow strong security standards before they connect to your network. Give them the tools to make security part of their work routine.

HOW TO ──────
PROTECT DEVICES

Whether employees or vendors use company-issued devices or their own when connecting remotely to your network, those devices should be secure. Follow these tips — and make sure your employees and vendors do as well:

Always change any pre-set router passwords and the default name of your router. And keep the router's software up to date; you may have to visit the router's website often to do so.

Consider enabling full-disk encryption for laptops and other mobile devices that connect remotely to your network. Check your operating system for this option, which will protect any data stored on the device if it's lost or stolen. This is especially important if the device stores any sensitive personal information.

Change smartphone settings to stop automatic connections to public Wi-Fi.

Keep up-to-date antivirus software on devices that connect to your network, including mobile devices.

CYBERSECURITY FOR
SMALL BUSINESS

HOW TO CONNECT
REMOTELY ──
TO THE NETWORK

Require employees and vendors to use secure connections when connecting remotely to your network. They should:

Use a router with WPA2 or WPA3 encryption when connecting from their homes. Encryption protects information sent over a network so that outsiders can't read it. WPA2 and WPA3 are the only encryption standards that will protect information sent over a wireless network.

Only use public Wi-Fi when also using a virtual private network (VPN) to encrypt traffic between their computers and the internet. Public Wi-Fi does not provide a secure internet connection on its own. Your employees can get a personal VPN account from a VPN service provider, or you may want to hire a vendor to create an enterprise VPN for all employees to use.

WHAT TO DO TO MAINTAIN SECURITY ──

Train your staff: Include information on secure remote access in regular trainings and new staff orientations.

Have policies covering basic cybersecurity, give copies to your employees, and explain the importance of following them.

Before letting any device — whether at an employee's home or on a vendor's network — connect to your network, make sure it meets your network's security requirements.

Tell your staff about the risks of public Wi-Fi.

Give your staff tools that will help maintain security:

- Require employees to use unique, complex network passwords and avoid unattended, open workstations.

- Consider creating a VPN for employees to use when connecting remotely to the business network.

- Require multi-factor authentication to access areas of your network that have sensitive information. This requires additional steps beyond logging in with a password — like a temporary code on a smartphone or a key that's inserted into a computer.

- If you offer Wi-Fi on your business premises for guests and customers, make sure it's separate from and not connected to your business network.

- Include provisions for security in your vendor contracts, especially if the vendor will be connecting remotely to your network.

Bibliography

American Public Power Association, *Public Power Cyber Incident Response Playbook*, American Public Power Association, August 2019, https://www.publicpower.org/system/files/documents/Public-Power-Cyber-Incident-Response-Playbook.pdf

Barker, W. et al., *Ransomware Risk Management: A Cybersecurity Framework Profile*, NIST, February, 2022, https://csrc.nist.gov/publications/detail/nistir/8374/final

Berris, P., Gaffney, J., *Ransomware and Federal Law: Cybercrime and Cybersecurity*, Congressional Research Service, October 5, 2021, https://crsreports.congress.gov/product/pdf/R/R46932

Canadian Centre for Cyber Security, *Ransomware Playbook*, Canadian Centre for Cyber Security, November 30, 2021, https://cyber.gc.ca/sites/default/files/2021-12/itsm00099-ransomware-playbook-2021-final3-en.pdf

Cybersecurity & Infrastructure Security Agency, *Ransomware Guide*, Cybersecurity & Infrastructure Security Agency, September 2020, https://www.cisa.gov/sites/default/files/publications/CISA_MS-ISAC_Ransomware%20Guide_S508C_.pdf

CyBOK Version 1.1.0, *The Cyber Security Body of Knowledge*, The National Cyber Security Centre, (2021), https://www.cybok.org/media/downloads/CyBOK_v1.1.0.pdf

Enisa, *Enisa Threat Landscape for Ransomware Attacks*, ENISA, July 29, 2022, https://www.enisa.europa.eu/publications/enisa-threat-landscape-for-ransomware-attacks

FATF, *Guidance on Digital Identity*, FATF, 2020, www.fatf-gafi.org/publications/documents/digital-identity-guidance.html

Federal Trade Commission, *Cybersecurity for Small Business*, Federal Trade Commission, May 2023, https://www.ftc.gov/system/files/attachments/cybersecurity-small-business/cybersecuirty_sb_factsheets_all.pdf

Federal Trade Commission, *Data Breach Response*, Federal Trade Commission, May 2019, https://www.ftc.gov/system/files/documents/plain-language/pdf-0154_data-breach-response-guide-for-business-042519-508.pdf

Federal Trade Commission, *Start with Security*, Federal Trade Commission, June 2015, https://www.ftc.gov/system/files/documents/plain-language/pdf0205-startwithsecurity.pdf

Institute for Security and Technology, *RTF Report: Combatting Ransomware, Institute for Security and Technology*, April 2021, https://securityandtechnology.org/wp-content/uploads/2021/09/IST-Ransomware-Task-Force-Report.pdf

Jones, C., *What is triple extortion ransomware?*, ITPro., October 13 2022, https://www.itpro.co.uk/security/ransomware/369222/what-is-triple-extortion-ransomware

King, S., *Ransomware Risk Management: 11 Essential Steps, Bank Info Security*, December 18, 2019, https://www.bankinfosecurity.com/blogs/ransomware-risk-management-11-essential-steps-p-2841

NIST, *SP 800-63 Digital Identity Guidelines*, National Institute of Standards and Technology, (2022), https://pages.nist.gov/800-63-4/sp800-63.html

NIST, *SP 800-63A Enrollment & Identity Proofing*, National Institute of Standards and Technology, (2023), https://pages.nist.gov/800-63-4/sp800-63a.html

NIST, *Getting Started with the NIST Cybersecurity Framework*, NIST, https://csrc.nist.gov/CSRC/media/Projects/cybersecurity-framework/documents/Framework_Quick%20Start_Guide.pdf
NIST, Small Business Cybersecurity Corner, NIST, https://www.nist.gov/system/files/documents/2022/02/17/Ransomware.pdf

Paulsen, C., Toth P, *Small Business Information Security: The Fundamentals*, NIST, November 2016, https://doi.org/10.6028/NIST.IR.7621r1

Sakellariadis, J., *Behind the Rise of Ransomware*, Atlantic Council, August 2022, https://www.atlanticcouncil.org/in-depth-research-reports/issue-brief/behind-the-rise-of-ransomware/

Sullivan, V., *Personal Liability for Directors Who Disregard Cybersecurity*, CPO Magazine, 2022, https://www.cpomagazine.com/cyber-security/personal-liability-for-directors-who-disregard-cybersecurity

Acknowledgments

I would like to acknowledge and thank all those who assisted me with this book, including Robert Carolina who wrote the *Law & Regulation* chapter in *The Cyber Security Body of Knowledge*. I would also like to acknowledge the cited public domain publications of the National Initiative for Cybersecurity Careers and Studies and the National Institute of Standards and Technology from which I have used significant portions.